101

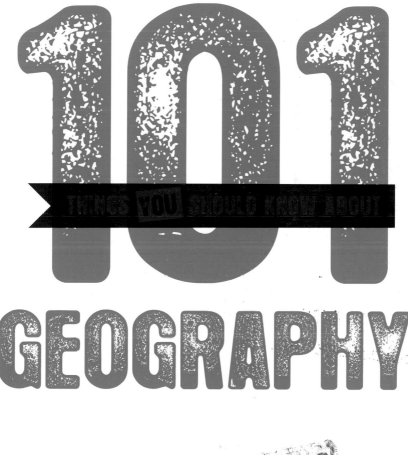

THINGS YOU SHOULD KNOW ABOUT

GEOGRAPHY

STERLING

New York

An Imprint of Sterling Publishing
387 Part Avenue South
New York, NY 10016

ISBN 978-1-4549-1044-2

Distributed in Canada by Sterling Publishing
c/o Canadian Manda Group, 165 Dufferin Street
Toronto, Ontario, Canada M6K 3H6
Distributed in the United Kingdom by GMC Distribution Services
Castle Place, 166 High Street, Lewes, East Sussex, England BN7 1XU
Distributed in Australia by Capricorn Link (Australia) Pty. Ltd.
P.O. Box 704, Windsor, NSW 2756, Australia

For information about custom editions, special sales, and premium and corporate
purchases, please contact Sterling Special Sales at 800-805-5489 or
specialsales@sterlingpublishing.com.

For Pulp Media Limited:
AUTHOR: Sonia Mehta (in association with Quadrum Solutions)
SERIES ART DIRECTOR: Allen Boe
SERIES EDITOR: Helena Caldon
DESIGN & EDITING: Quadrum Solutions
PUBLISHER: James Tavendale

IMAGES courtesy of www.shutterstock.com

Manufactured in China

2 4 6 8 10 9 7 5 3 1

www.sterlingpublishing.com

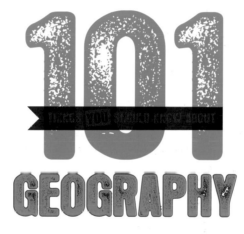

101

THINGS YOU SHOULD KNOW ABOUT

GEOGRAPHY

STERLING

New York

INTRODUCTION

"Everywhere has been where it is ever since it was first put there. It's called geography," said Terry Pratchett, author of Wyrd Sisters. True. And if we scratch the surface and get a little deeper there's a whole new world out there to discover. This book, ***101 Things You Should Know About Geography,*** attempts to take you through all those enchanting, fascinating, and sometimes downright mind-boggling places that your geography teacher forgot to mention.

For example, take the dancing Northern Lights that are caused when atmospheric particles from the Sun sneak into the Earth's atmosphere, or the man-made hole that is seven and a half miles deep, or the exploding lakes—Monoun, Nyos, and Kivu. Did your geography textbooks miss out on these? Probably.

But it's still not too late to find out what our Earth, its surroundings, and its habitat are all about. So go ahead, unravel the mysteries and find out amazing facts that you never knew existed. These facts—we bet—are far stranger than fiction. Happy reading!

PLANETS

ASTEROID

BLACK HOLE

SUN

SATURN

JUPITER

PLUTO

DWARF PLANET

MERCURY

NEPTUNE

TITAN

 SOLAR SYSTEM

EARTH

MARS

METEORITE

URANUS

EARTH

1. THE HOTTEST PLANET

The closer a planet is to the Sun, the hotter it should be, right? By that logic, Mercury, the planet that is closest to the Sun, should be the hottest. But as bizarre as it may sound, it is not so. In fact, this honor goes to Venus, the planet that comes after Mercury. Strange? Read on to find out why.

The answer lies in the different atmospheres of these planets. The atmosphere of any planet plays a very important role in determining the temperature of a planet. Ours does a good job of keeping the Earth warm and cozy enough to sustain life. But things are different on Mercury, which rotates and revolves closest to the Sun. During the day, the side of the planet facing the Sun gets heated to approximately 800° F and at night, when that side of the planet is not facing the Sun, the temperature dips to −315° F. However, what makes the difference on Mercury is the atmosphere responsible for trapping all the heat which is absent from around Mercury.

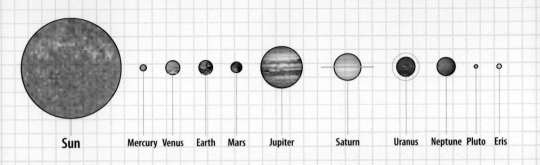

Sun   Mercury   Venus   Earth   Mars   Jupiter   Saturn   Uranus   Neptune Pluto   Eris

Venus, on the other hand, gets toasted to 863° F during the day, which is maintained throughout the night. Now that's really hot, isn't it? This is because like Earth, Venus' atmosphere also traps heat, causing Venus to be hotter than Mercury. The atmosphere around Venus is made up of carbon dioxide (CO_2), which traps all the heat.

Hence, Venus is the hottest plant in our solar system, and not Mercury.

FAST FACT . . .

The best way to remember all the planets of our solar system in their correct sequence is to memorize the sentence, "My Very Educated Mother Just Served Us Nachos." The first letter of every word gives you a hint to naming the planets in their order – Mercury, Venus, Earth, Mars, Jupiter, Saturn, Uranus, and Neptune.

2. NAMING PLUTO

Until 2006, Pluto was considered a planet. Post that, after various debates and discussions, it was decided that this particular celestial mass doesn't fulfill all the requirements of a "planet," and is no longer considered one. But do you know how Pluto was christened? Here's a peek at the elaborate process that preceded the naming of Pluto.

It all began in 1905 when American astronomer, Percival Lowell, noticed that the gravitational pull of a heavy "something" was disturbing the orbits of Neptune and Uranus. Unfortunately, due to the lack of technology

FAST FACT . . .
Pluto is the only recognized celestial body in our solar system that crosses the orbits of another planet (Neptune).

in those days, Lowell couldn't find concrete evidence about this mysterious "something." He decided to call it Planet X.

Lowell died in 1916, but on February 18, 1930, 23-year-old Clyde W. Tombaugh from the Lowell Observatory finally managed to reveal the identity of Planet X. He did it with the help of a 13-inch telescope. Planet X's discovery was declared to the public on March 13, 1930.

Now that the "something" had been identified, it was time to give it a more respectable name than "Planet X." Everyone began suggesting names for this newly found planet. Finally, 11-year-old Venetia Burney (from Oxford, England) came up with the name "Pluto."

Pluto was deemed an appropriate name because of the similarities between the characteristics of the planet and of the Greek God Pluto

FAST FACT . . .
In 1930, Walt Disney created a cartoon character called Pluto, who was influential in naming the planet.

(the God of the Underworld). The planet had an unfavorable surface condition. Moreover, the initials of Percival Lowell (PL) made up the first two letters of Pluto.
It couldn't get better than that, could it?

FAST FACT . . .
When the International Astronomical Union (IAU) came up with the definition of a planet in 2006, scientists realized that Pluto didn't fulfill all the criteria of being a "planet." Hence, it is now known as a "dwarf planet."

3. ALIEN ROCKS

Our astronomers and researchers put in a great deal of effort to find out more about our immediate neighbors by sending unmanned spaceships to Mars. But did you know that a good deal of the information about Mars can be found on Earth itself? That's because our planet has been sprinkled with Martian rocks of various sizes.

Environmental conditions on Mars are very harsh. It's a planet that's hot and houses many volcanoes, and sometimes the explosive eruptions from these volcanoes are so massive that little rocks shoot out and land on Earth.

Till date, scientists have found around 65 Martian rocks on Earth. Most of them were found in the Antarctica or the Sahara Desert. The oldest Martian rock is 4.5 billion years old. It's called "Allan Hills 84001" because it was found in Allan Hills, Antarctica, on December 27, 1984.

Studies of such Martian rocks have revealed that Mars, was once a wet planet. The rocks, dating from 4.5 billion years old to 600 million years old, also tell us the story of how Mars, as a planet, has changed. The latest meteorite suspected to be from

Mars is called NWA 7034. It was discovered in the Sahara Desert. It is about 2.1 billion years old.

The next time you come across an odd-looking rock; think before tossing it away; perhaps you're holding a piece of Mars in your hand!

FAST FACT . . .

The largest volcano in the solar system is situated on Mars. It's called Olympus Mons and is about 14 miles in height and 370 miles wide.

4. THE LARGEST PLANET

Jupiter is the largest planet in our solar system, and it looks like this position has given the planet some sense of responsibility. Perhaps that's why it keeps a check on the debris that float around and revolve in our solar system.

The radius of Jupiter is 43,440.7 miles. That's what makes it a huge planet. But with great mass, comes great gravity. Any asteroids or debris that are floating around Jupiter

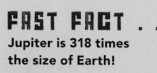

FAST FACT . . .
Jupiter is 318 times the size of Earth!

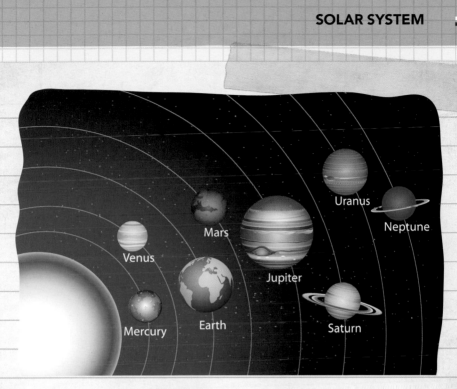

get sucked in due to its gravity. However, this works as a good thing, because Jupiter protects us by sucking in many asteroids that would otherwise come hurtling right at us.

This action was observed by a Frenchman called Pierre Simon, who noticed that a comet heading for Earth disappeared into Jupiter's atmosphere.

Pierre Simon

5. FLOATING SATURN

Saturn could float on water. Of course, the vessel we would need to test this fact would have to be rather massive. However, if the swish of a magical wand could conjure a bowl that size, we would be able to see Saturn floating in it! Having a tough time believing that? Don't worry, there's a perfectly logical explanation.

Saturn is 80 percent larger than the Earth, but if the two planets were to be dropped into an ocean, the Earth would sink right to the bottom while Saturn would happily float on top. This is because of Saturn's

FAST FACT . . .
Saturn rotates very fast. While one day on Earth is made up of 24 hours, on Saturn, a day is just 10 hours long!

density, which is 1/10th that of Earth and 2/3rd that of water. Since Saturn's density is less than that of water, it wouldn't sink.

Apart from this, even though Saturn is the second largest planet in the solar system (after Jupiter) its gravitational pull is almost equal to that of the Earth. This air-headedness of Saturn has caused it to be called a "gas giant."

Saturn lacks a solid surface. This means that there is no land on Saturn. Its surface is a murky gaseous platform and the distinction between Saturn's surface and the atmosphere isn't clear.

The next time you think of Saturn, think of a giant ball of thick gases floating on water.

> **FAST FACT . . .**
> Traces of water are also present on Saturn because of the presence of hydrogen and oxygen in its atmosphere. But all the water on this planet is frozen due to its cold temperature.

6. SEASONS ON URANUS

A season on Uranus lasts for 24 years. To top that, a day on Uranus is much shorter than a day on Earth—it is just 17 hours and 14 minutes. That means that Uranus completes one rotation faster than Earth, yet one side of the planet is closer to the Sun for a much longer period of time. Here's why.

Uranus is tilted at its axis. It appears as though it has almost toppled on one side.
It is tilted by 98°. When it rotates, one side faces the Sun for 24 years while the other side is in the dark for the same amount of time.

FAST FACT . . .
The first planet to be discovered by a telescope was Uranus.

Scientists believe that when the solar system was initially formed, a huge heavenly body—perhaps as big as the Earth—bumped into Uranus and caused it to topple, which is why it has been revolving and rotating in the same position ever since.

7. THE SUN DOESN'T BURN

Now that statement is really hard to believe, considering how hot we feel during the summer. If the Sun is not a big ball of fire up in the sky, then where is all the heat coming from?

the nuclear fusion that is taking place in its core. During this nuclear fusion, two protons collide with each other with such strength that they get stuck, or "fuse" together. This fusion lets out huge amounts of energy. When this energy gets released, it heats things up.

The Sun, which is actually a star, is not burning. If you think about it carefully, you would realize that it would be illogical for the Sun to burn, because there is no oxygen in space, and oxygen is necessary for anything to burn. Hence, the Sun is most definitely not "burning." The Sun's "glow" comes from

FAST FACT . . .
The Sun accounts for 99.58 percent of the mass of the solar system.

8. DWARF PLANETS

We all know the story of Pluto and how it was stripped of its prestigious status as a planet and degraded to that of a dwarf planet. But, most people are unaware of the existence of four other dwarf planets orbiting in our solar system: Ceres, Eris, Makemake, and Haumea.

In 2006, the International Astronomical Union (IAU) coined the term "dwarf planet" and explained how they are different from actual planets. Following this clarification, Pluto got pushed into the category of a dwarf planet. We then discovered that Pluto had company! It wasn't the only dwarf planet in our solar system.

In 1801, an asteroid called Ceres was spotted orbiting in the asteroid belt between Mars and Jupiter. Like Pluto, it was considered to be a planet for about 50 years, after which it was categorized as an asteroid. It was only in 2006, when IAU coined the term dwarf planet, that Ceres gained entry into this club.

In 2005, scientists had begun to debate about the presence of a 10th planet in our solar system—Eris. But like Pluto, even this was considered to be a dwarf planet in 2006. The other two dwarf planets—Makemake and Haumea—are located beyond Neptune's orbit. Makemake made it into the list of dwarf planets in 2006, followed by Haumea in 2008.

FAST FACT . . .

A dwarf planet is round because of its gravitation pull, but it has other celestial bodies—like asteroids or another planet—in its orbit.

9. SLOWING EARTH

The Earth is slowing down. Back in the day, when dinosaurs roamed the Earth, a day was about 23 hours long. Today, our planet takes an additional hour to complete one rotation. Does that mean that the Earth is slowing down? Technically, yes.

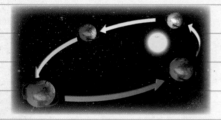

During this time, the moon is pushed farther away from the Earth, which directly affects the rotation of the Earth.

Another factor is the melting of the polar ice caps, causing water to collect around the Equator. Scientists believe that it could be a contributing factor to the slowing down of the Earth's speed.

Though the slowing down of the Earth is a million times slower than a snail—1.4 milliseconds/100 years, it cannot be disputed that the Earth is indeed slowing down. Why? The moon is partially to blame.

Here's why. The moon is responsible for the tidal waves on Earth, and forms a tidal bulge. This creates a slight distortion in the shape of the Earth during the tides.

FAST FACT . . .
The Earth takes exactly 23 hours, 56 minutes, and 4 seconds to complete one rotation.

10. THE EARTH ISN'T ROUND

Though many have flippantly referred to the shape of the Earth as round, it actually isn't! While you aren't entirely wrong to think of it as round, you aren't entirely right either. Our planet is slightly flattened at the poles. Such a shape is called a spheroid.

The first one to propose that the Earth is actually an oblate spheroid was Sir Isaac Newton (of the falling apple fame).
This means that our planet flaunts a slight bulge at the Equator and is flattened at the poles.

This is because of the speed at which our planet is revolving. It is similar in the bulge that appears in the middle of a blob of clay on a potter's wheel due to the spinning motion.

FAST FACT . . .
The amount of ice in Antarctica is equal to the amount of water in the Atlantic Ocean.

Also, mass is not evenly distributed on the surface of the Earth where the vast water body is sprinkled with solid land.
All this keeps the Earth from being perfectly round.

FAST FACT . . .
Due to the bulge at the Equator it is 13 miles further away from the core than the poles.

11. ASTEROID STALKER

There's an asteroid that's stalking the Earth. We have company while we orbit the Sun. Our constant companion is a Trojan asteroid called 2010TK7. But don't worry, this large rock is not likely to bump into us any time soon.

On July 27, 2011, NASA (National Aeronautics and Space Administration) found an asteroid that was accompanying our planet during its revolution. It was discovered by Martin Connors at the Athabasca University in Canada. The asteroid came to be named as 2010TK7 because the mission to reveal more about this rock began in October 2010.

FAST FACT . . .
Trojan asteroids are also found in the orbits of Jupiter, Neptune, and Mars.

What are the chances of this meteor bringing us to an apocalyptic end? It's not very high, and for the foreseeable future, we are well out of harm's way.

FAST FACT . . .

Asteroids are large chunks of rock that were leftover after the solar system was formed. They are like the little pebbles that remain after the construction work is complete.

As it usually happens with such asteroids, it will lose its gravity and get blown away in a short span of time (1,000—10,000 years).

The Trojan asteroid, which is 328 yards wide, revolves far away from our planet. It revolves around an empty space in an oval-ish orbit. It silently follows the Earth as it goes about doing its daily rotational and revolutionary business.

Scientist expect that that 2010TK7 will meet a similar fate. As of now, the asteroid is close to the Earth. It will be at its farthest position in the year 2209 and will come close to the Earth again in 2400.

12. RING-SHAPED CRATER

Around 200 million years ago, an asteroid hit the Earth. That's how the story of the Manicouagan crater began. Surprisingly, the place of impact is not a round depression, but a ring-shaped one that has been filled with water to form a lake.

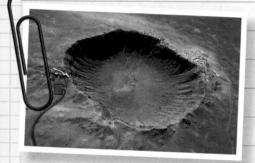

When the asteroid hit the Earth, what probably happened was that it formed a round crater. However, the underground fluid pressure in this area was very high. This means that the water underneath kept pushing the land up. Slowly, but steadily, the central part of this crater started rising. Water filled the surrounding area, giving it the appearance of a ring-like structure. This fascinating structure is clearly visible in photographs taken from outer space.

The Manicouagan crater is situated in the northern part of Quebec. Scientists believe that it was created about 214 million years ago. The total area is more than 45 miles in diameter. While the outer part is depressed, the center is raised in the form of a plateau, which makes the crater look like a ring.

Due to the impact, the timeline of rocks in this area was reset. While rocks in the neighboring areas are Precambrian rocks, the rocks of the Manicouagan crater are Triassic rocks. This means that the rocks in the surrounding area are much older than the rocks in the crater itself.

FAST FACT . . .
Precambrian rocks date back to around 4 billion – 540 million years ago. Triassic rocks are 250 million years old.

13. TITAN'S LAKES

The Earth boasts of being the only planet with water, but it cannot boast of being the only celestial structure with lakes. Saturn's moon, Titan, is also said to have a number of lakes. However, these lakes do not contain water. So if there's no water on Titan, what on Earth, I mean Saturn, are these lakes filled with?

In 1995, thanks to the Hubble Telescope, scientists discovered that Titan, one of Saturn's moons, was dotted with lakes, rivers, and seas.
They looked identical to the ones we have here on Earth, except that they weren't filled with water. Scientists were certain because the temperature on Titan is around -297° F, which is well below the freezing point of water. This means that if it were water, it would be solid, not liquid.

Closer inspection revealed that the lakes were filled with liquid hydrocarbons such as methane and ethane. This is because of the atmosphere around Titan contains highly toxic gases — nitrogen and methane.

It has also been observed that the lakes are absolutely still during the winter when the climate is cold. Scientists are expecting the climate to warm up around the year 2017, when strong winds will cause waves in these lakes.

Researchers are banking on the formation of waves in these bodies of liquids because, by observing the waves, scientists will be able to gauge the changes in the speed of wind.

FAST FACT . . .
While the discovery of lakes had thrilled the researchers, some scientists fear that the lakes might dry up because they are not getting replenished by rains.

14. HEAVENLY SHOWERS!

We know that the Earth is the only planet that has water, but did you know that other planets receive rainfall too? If it doesn't rain water, what rains on other planets? Cats and dogs? Not really.

We're used to seeing the different forms of water pouring down on our planet—be it snow, rain, or hail. But Earth is the only planet in the solar system with water. So what is it that "rains" on the other planets?

Since several toxic chemicals like ethane, methane, and sulphuric acid make up the atmosphere of other planets, it is the liquid form of these toxins that splashes down on other planets. Just the thought of it makes you shudder, doesn't it?

To add to the misery of these planets, they not only experience regular drizzles, but also face storms and hurricanes that are several hundred times more violent than the ones we witness here on Earth. Imagine being caught in one of those!

Take the case of the Great Red Spot on Jupiter. This spot is actually a hurricane that seems to have lasted for 500 years now. It was discovered when Galileo first pointed his telescope at Jupiter way back in the early

1600s, so for all we know, it might even be older. Right now, with meteors raining on the largest planet, Jupiter seems to be in the most discomfort.

FAST FACT . . .

Venus is a planet that's considered to be just like Earth except for the fact that it has sulphuric acid instead of water. When this acid rains down, it evaporates even before it touches the ground.

15. BLACK HOLES

Black holes are the black splotches that scientists see in space. You can't actually "see" a black hole, because it's so dark, but its presence can be affirmed by the behavior of other objects in its vicinity. What makes a black hole so black? Let's find out.

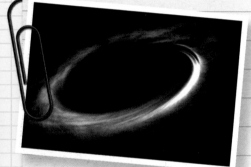

Imagine a celestial body that is a thousand times larger than the Earth, shrinking down to the size of New York City. Because a star which was so large and heavy at one point of time has suddenly contracted so much and become so tiny, the gravitational pull of that star becomes tremendous. The star

Stars, like our Sun, are made of fuel—gases like hydrogen and nitrogen—that aid their process of nuclear fusion and allow them to keep burning and creating energy. But, like most fuel-driven objects, the fuel runs out at some point of time. Once this happens, the star begins to shrink. It grows smaller and smaller until it becomes as small as an atom.

FAST FACT . . .

There are many sizes of black holes. Supermassive black holes are found at the center of the galaxies usually millions of times the mass of our Sun, whereas stellar black holes float around anywhere.

begins to collapse into itself. During this process, it starts attracting everything that's around. It begins to resemble a vacuum cleaner that sucks everything inside, even light.

This is why black holes appear so black – they literally suck all the light in.

FAST FACT . . .

Scientists have discovered that black holes are very noisy. That's because they pull in so many objects that there is a constant gurgling sound around them.

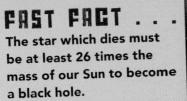

FAST FACT . . .

The star which dies must be at least 26 times the mass of our Sun to become a black hole.

16. SOLAR STORMS

The Sun, which is generally very well-behaved and obliging when it comes to sustaining life on Earth, sometimes sends a large wave of magnetic particles into the solar system. This is called a solar storm, and can upset climatic conditions on Earth.

There are certain spots on the Sun's surface that look like dark spots when viewed through a telescope. These are cold regions on the surface of the Sun. It is quite strange that a celestial body as hot as the Sun should have cold spots, isn't it? Solar storms occur every 11 years, caused by these cold regions. They are really huge magnetic waves that can disrupt radio transmissions and mobile networks.

FAST FACT . . .
During one such violent solar storm on March 13, 1989, power across Quebec was knocked out for more than nine hours.

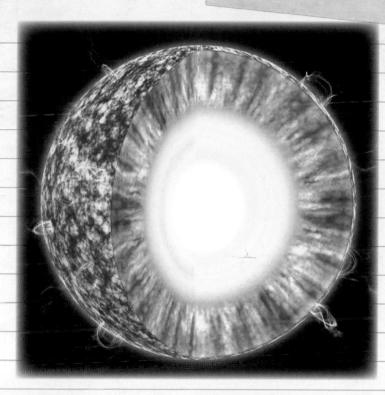

There is a slow build-up of magnetic energy in the form of a cloud on the Sun's surface. This build up continues until the Sun just can't take it anymore, and the cloud explodes, sending huge magnetic waves into the solar system.

FAST FACT . . .
The biggest solar flare on the Sun is about ten times the size of Earth.

MOUNTAINS

SARGASSO

TECTONIC PLATES

OCEAN

ALASKA

MT. FUJI

MOUNT CHIMBORAZO

SARGASSO

TECTONIC PLATES

NAMIB DESERT

LANDFORMS AND REGIONS

TIMBUKTU

LAKE

KOLA SUPERDEEP BOREHOLE

17. THE SARGASSO SEA

Could you imagine a sea that does not border any land? As bizarre this sounds, this is true. The Sargasso Sea has only ocean currents to demarcate its borders. How did a sea land up in the middle of an ocean? Here's how.

The Sargasso Sea is a 2,000,000 square-mile, ellipse-shaped region in the middle of North Atlantic Ocean. It is set amidst rotating ocean currents. Marking its northern boundary is the North Atlantic current, to the east is the Canary current, to the south is the North Atlantic Equatorial current, and to its west is the Gulf Stream. Because the boundaries of the Sargasso Sea are not solid, they keep shifting and changing as the currents move.

How was a sea amidst an ocean discovered, though? It happened because geologists spotted this

FAST FACT . . .

A doldrum is an area found 5° north or south of the Equator which experiences a total lack of wind.

vast patch of sea covered with free-floating seaweed called sargassum. Even though this patch was in the middle of the ocean, scientists decided to demarcate it and name it the Sargasso Sea.

This sea is home to several marine species. Turtles lay their eggs here, using the sargassum seaweed as mats and nurseries, where hatchlings have food and shelter. You can even find several threatened or endangered eels, white marlin, porbeagle shark, and dolphin fish. Humpback whales also migrate here every year.

This sea has been associated with many shipwrecks. While many believe that it is because ships get tangled in the web of weeds, but the real reason is the lack of wind in this area, because it is situated in one of the doldrums of the Atlantic Ocean.

18. GREAT BARRIER REEF

Here's a horrifying detail about the Earth's largest natural structure. The Great Barrier Reef, which is situated in the Coral Sea, off the coast of Queensland in Australia, is in danger of being eaten by a starfish. But could a structure as big as the Great Barrier Reef really fall prey to a starfish?

The Great Barrier Reef spans over more than 1,600 miles and is made up of a billion tiny organisms called Coral Polyps. The reef began forming very slowly around 50 million years ago.

Then tectonic forces began to force Australia to inch towards it, triggering the growth of the reefs. That's because the polyps need a very specific environment and temperature for growth. Today, the reef stands as a cluster of 900 islands that can be viewed even from outer space.

While we take great pride in this majestic structure, a threat to its very existence has been discovered—the crown-of-thorns starfish. These starfish are releasing their digestive juices onto the corals, which is causing them to dissolve.

Researchers believe that the population of this particular starfish is on the rise because of an ecological imbalance due to pollution. Mollusks, certain fish, and worms feed on this starfish. However, because of oil spills and other marine pollution, the predators of crown-of-thorns starfish are declining, leading to an increase in the starfish's numbers.

Unless the ecological balance is restored, this beautiful natural wonder may actually disappear sometime in the near future.

> ## FAST FACT . . .
> **The Great Barrier Reef houses about 1,500 species of tropical fish, 400 types of corals, 200 types of birds, and 20 types of reptiles, amongst many other unidentified species.**

19. KOLA SUPERDEEP BOREHOLE

The Kola Superdeep Borehole is as deep as 20 Empire State Buildings. It is also man-made! This ginormous hole was drilled by the Russians in an attempt to study the structure of the Earth's crust. Actually, the Kola Superdeep Borehole isn't a single hole; it is several holes that branch out from one single hole.

The project that dealt with Kola Superdeep Borehole began in 1962 by USSR's Interdepartmental Scientific Council for the study of the Earth's Interior and Superdeep Drilling, but it was only in 1970, after detailed research and studies, that the drilling finally started.

FAST FACT . . .
The liquid core of the Earth is about 3,959 miles from the surface and about 10,832° F, which is as hot as the surface of the Sun!

Oceanic crust
Continental crust
Lithosphere
Asthenosphere
Upper mantle
Lower mantle
Outer core
Inner core

The single hole, which is the deepest, is called SG-3. It is only 9 inches in diameter, but is around 7.5 miles deep into the Earth's crust.

As the hole deepened, scientists made remarkable discoveries. One of these was the discovery of perfectly preserved microscopic fossils at a depth of about 4.16 miles. It was also observed that the temperature rose very quickly as the hole deepened. Researchers did not expect temperatures to rise above 212°F (100°C), but 7.5 miles into the crust, the temperature was about 356°F (180°C).

FAST FACT . . .

In 1957 the United States also attempted to drill a hole into the crust. The project was called Project Mohole. Unfortunately it was canceled due to the lack of funding.

The drilling was halted in 1994 when the hole was about seven miles deep, because of the unexpected high temperatures. Even though it is an achievement for mankind to have drilled a hole this deep, we have still barely managed to scratch the surface of the Earth's crust, which is more than 50 miles deep.

20. Å

Yes, that's the name of a village in Norway! While it's pretty...er...short, the little circle on its head makes it somewhat unique, doesn't it? But wait a minute before you nail that thought. There are actually a handful of other places that go by the same name.

Å is a tiny little fishing village situated in Lofoten, Norway. While it was initially just a quaint little village occupied by fishermen, Å has now become a tourist destination thanks to its 19th century storehouses, boathouses, farmhouses, and other commercial buildings that constitute the Norwegian Fishing Village Museum.

The fishing village of Å, Norway

But this is not the only Å on the world map. There are seven other places, all in Norway itself, that are named Å. What's more, in the Scandinavian language, Å denotes a river.

While we have the famous Å as the shortest name, there are other places that have one-letter names. There's I, a village in China, Ú, a place in Madagascar, and Y, a settlement in Alaska—to name a few.

Take the case of a river in the USA called D. Comically, D is one of the shortest rivers in the world as well. D, in Oregon, USA, is only 440 feet long. There's also a river called E in Scotland which is about 6 miles in length.

It's a pretty lazy way to name a place, don't you think?

FAST FACT . . .
Å is also the name of a village in Sweden that has a population of about 200. There are 12 other places in Sweden called Å.

21. MOUNT CHIMBORAZO

Mount Chimborazo is the point on Earth that is closest to the moon. Confused? Logically, the highest peak in the world should be the closest to the Moon, given that the Moon is safely tucked behind fluffy clouds up in the sky, right? But hold on a second before raising your eyebrow—let us tell you why this isn't so.

Mt. Chimborazo

The height of Mount Chimborazo, situated in Andes in Eucador, South America, is 20,561 feet, while that of Mount Everest is 29,035 feet. So how is it possible to be closer to the moon if we stand on Mount Chimborazo than if we stand on the top of Mount Everest?

Take a guess as to why this might be the case. The answer here has already been discussed in this book. The myth about our world being perfectly round has already been busted. We know that contrary to common belief, it is an oblate spheroid, which means that it bulges from around the Equator and is flattened at the poles. Mount Chimborazo is situated on one such bulge.

Due to this, the base of Mount Chimborazo is 1.5 miles higher than that of Mount Everest. This is why the peak of this mountain comes much closer to the moon than the peak of Mount Everest.

FAST FACT . . .

Mount Chimborazo is barely 1° south of the Equator while Mount Everest is 28° north.

22. GLACIERS

We know that the northern and southern caps of the Earth are frozen. We are also aware that higher altitudes all over our Earth are cold and icy. Glaciers—solid, frozen expanses of water—are found in these places. Such places cover 10 Percent of the Earth's surface.

The largest ice cap in the world is the southern ice cap, Antarctica. At the North Pole we have Greenland, which is a considerably smaller ice cap, but a substantial chunk nonetheless.

FAST FACT . . .
Glaciers move very slowly, but cause a lot of friction when they move. This can result in soil erosion and even in the formation of glaciated valleys.

In total, glaciers cover an area of 5.8 million square miles, which is a little less than twice the size of the USA! In fact, glaciers cover more than 30,000 square miles of the USA itself, with most of the glaciers obviously situated in Alaska.

FAST FACT . . .
Glaciers provide around 470 billion gallons of water to Washington State in the USA every year.

ability to "move." Because of their huge mass, they flow like very slow rivers. The record for the fastest glacial travel is held by the Kutiah Glacier in Pakistan. It raced about 7.5 miles in three months. Quite the Usain Bolt of glaciers, don't you think?

What is fascinating is that more than 70 percent of the fresh water reserves of the Earth are frozen in these ice caps. It is estimated that if all land ice melted, the sea level would rise by approximately 230 feet!

Another thing that makes glaciers more than just mountains of ice is their unique

FAST FACT . . .
Glaciers are made of ice that has minimum air pockets. The snow which is yet to become a glacier is called a firn.

23. SHRINKING OCEANS

It has been theorized that a long, long time ago (about 200 million years to be precise) all the land on Earth was actually just a big mass called Pangaea. Because of the constant movement of the tectonic plates below the surface of the Earth, the continents began to drift apart, as though they were angry with each other. However, the continents seem to have reconciled recently, and seem to be coming closer together.

There are 12 rigid plates under the Earth's land and the sea beds. These plates are constantly colliding with each other, making continents shift ever so slightly.

Scientists predict that in the next 20 million years, Australia will have moved much closer to the Equator. Studies also reveal that the Atlantic Ocean is widening, while the Pacific Ocean is shrinking.

FAST FACT . . .
The Alps and the Himalayas were mountain ranges that were created by the collision of the continental drift.

The idea of the continental drift was first proposed by German meteorologist and polar explorer Alfred Wegener in 1915 in his book "The Origin of the Continents and Oceans." However, it wasn't very popular in those days. Gradually, scientists started opening up to the idea, and the notion was accepted in the 1960s.

Pangaea

Eurasia

North America

South America

Africa

Antarctica

Australia

24. EXPLODING LAKES

Did you ever think that a lake could explode? Some lakes seem to have a rather nasty temper. There are three such exploding lakes—Monoun, Nyos, and Kivu (all in Africa)—on our planet. This makes the chances of a peaceful boat ride on any of these rather slim. But why and how do these lakes explode?

The first time this phenomenon was observed was on Lake Monoun in 1984. It killed 37 people living nearby.

This bizarre phenomenon usually occurs when lakes are situated over a weak spot or a crack on the Earth. Magma from the Earth's interior slowly creeps up in such areas. Lakes Monoun and Nyos were formed due to such explosions. A crater gets formed when the crust explodes, and as years go by, these craters are filled with water, turning them into lakes.

There have been several folk tales and legends about demons residing in these lakes due to their explosive nature. It isn't difficult to see why! Imagine taking a leisurely walk by the lake when BAM! It explodes, killing everything within a 1-mile radius!

Under the lake, the weak spot still persists, through which large amounts of CO_2 leak out. For some time, the leaked gas remains under the water, but a tiny disturbance, such as a strong gust of wind, or a slight landslide, is enough to make this gas-filled water explode—somewhat like a bottle of champagne.

FAST FACT . . .

A natural explosion occurred in Lake Nyos in 1986, where many villagers living around the lake lost their lives.

25. THE MARIANA TRENCH

The Mariana Trench, which lies in the Pacific Ocean, is deeper than Mount Everest put upside down. Apart from being unique because of its depth, the Trench is different because it is located on the oldest seabed in the world.

The Mariana Trench is located in the western Pacific Ocean. It is about 1,580 miles long with an average width of 43 miles and is 6.8 miles deep. The deepest point on the Mariana Trench is the Challenger Deep, which is nearly 7 miles deep. Yet what is interesting is that even though it is the deepest trench on the Earth's surface, its bottom isn't the point of the Earth that is closest to the core.

Once again, we can blame this on the imperfect roundness of the Earth. Since the Earth bulges slightly around the Equator, and the Mariana Trench is located near the Equator, it isn't the closest to the center of the Earth.

The seabed on which the Mariana Trench is located is about 180 million years old. It is made of a kind of yellowish, viscous substance that was formed from the decay of shells, sea animals, and phytoplankton.

Due to the depth and its peculiar surroundings, the Mariana Trench is known to support the growth of

FAST FACT . . .
The Mariana Trench was discovered by HMS Challenger in 1875.

FAST FACT . . .

James Cameron, a National Geographic explorer and movie director, visited the Mariana Trench in 2012. Sadly, he couldn't capture images due to a hydraulic fluid leak.

unusual sea life. Scientists have observed that organisms in this part of the world live longer than their counterparts living in other parts.

FAST FACT . . .

The water pressure on the floor of the trench is more than 8 tons per square inch, the equivalent of having 50 jumbo jets piled on top of a person.

26. THE SALTIER OCEAN

If you were to go around the world tasting ocean water, you would conclude that the Atlantic Ocean is the saltiest. But what could possibly cause one ocean to be saltier than another? Could it be just coincidence? There is a reason behind it, and here it is.

The Pacific Ocean is the largest ocean in the world. A larger ocean should necessarily mean that there is more salt, right? The salinity of an ocean depends upon its rate of evaporation. Oceans which have a higher rate of evaporation are saltier. This is because though the water evaporates, the salt gets left behind.

This is exactly what happens with the Atlantic Ocean.

The North Atlantic Ocean water is the saltiest because of the currents that bring water in to this part of the ocean. The Gulf Stream, which contributes to this ocean, originates in the very warm area of the Gulf of Mexico.

FAST FACT . . .
The highest salinity of the North Atlantic Ocean is 35 percent.

FAST FACT . . .

Rainfalls, rivers, and the melting of glacial ice are factors that reduce the salinity of water in oceans.

On the other hand, near the coast of Canada, the precipitation (or rainfall) is high, which dilutes the salty water and adds fresh water to the Atlantic Ocean. Hence, the salinity decreases near the coast of Canada.

This area has a very high rate of evaporation, which in turn leads to the increased salinity of the North Atlantic Ocean.

27. DING DONG TOWN

There is a town called Ding Dong, which is situated in Bell County, Texas. Doesn't it seem like it's taken right out of a rather "punny" book? It's true, though. But hold on before you start grinning—there's an equally amusing history behind the name. Settle down and read on about it right here!

SOUTH DAKOTA
★ USA ★

Common sense dictates that Ding Dong's presence in Bell County cannot possibly be a coincidence. Surely the two must have something to do with each other? This isn't the case though. The town got its name in around 1930, when two residents of the area, Zulis Bell, and his nephew, Bert Bell, bought and ran a country store. They decided to paint a sign on their newly acquired store. They hired a talented painter called C.C. Hoover for the job. Hoover fancied himself as a creative man, and was not content with merely painting a mundane, conventional sign. So, in addition to the sign, he painted two bells, perhaps to denote their surname, and wrote "ding" under one, and "dong" under the other.

Because of this amusing board the entire community and area came to be known as Ding

FAST FACT . . .

There is also a town called Pringle in South Dakota. 96 people reside there.

Dong. The town is so small that at one point in time, it had a population of only 22. Today, the population stands at 667.

28. GROWING MT. EVEREST

It looks like being the tallest peak on Earth isn't enough for Mount Everest. Determined to reach for the stars, Mount Everest actually grows by 0.15 inches every year. This mountain is not willing to give up the prestigious position of the tallest peak in the world any time soon! How is it growing, though?

A long time ago, the Indian subcontinent was separated from the Eurasian continent by a large sea. Then, around 50 million years ago, India slowly began inching toward the larger continent at the rate of four inches per year.

Tenzing Norgay

FAST FACT . . .

Tenzing Norgay (an Indian who accompanied Edmund Hillary, the first man to scale Mount Everest on his historic journey) didn't know how to write, but he could speak seven different languages.

Back then, there were no mountain ranges bordering India on the north. It was only when India finally bumped into

FAST FACT . . .
People started attempting to scale Mount Everest only after 1921, when Tibet opened its borders to outsiders.

and and collided with the rest of the landmass that the Himalayas were created. The tectonic plates under the continents kept colliding, giving rise to the Himalayan range.

Even today, this tectonic plate movement continues, making the Himalayas grow! Using the Global Positioning System (GPS), scientists have found that the Everest rises .1576 inches (about four millimeters) every year!

FAST FACT . . .
On May 29, 1953, Edmund Hillary and Tenzing Norgay were the first people to reach the summit of Mount Everest.

29. THE SALTIEST LAKE

While the North Atlantic Ocean takes the cake when it comes to the salinity of oceans, when it comes to lakes, the Great Salt Lake of Utah bags the position of Miss Salty. Yes, this lake is the saltiest water body on Earth.

FAST FACT . . .
Due to the large concentration of salt present in this Great Salt Lake, swallowing even a little water from the lake can make you sick.

We have already established that the salinity of a water body depends upon the amount of water that evaporates. The Great Salt Lake of Utah is the shallowest lake with the maximum amount of surface area.

Its area is 1,730 square miles and its depth is merely 33 feet. This means that a lot of water evaporates, leaving behind concentrated salt.

FAST FACT . . .
The Great Salt Lake of Utah is home to salt-loving micro-organisms that give a pinkish hue to the lake.

Also, because such a huge amount of water evaporates from the lake during the summers, its boundaries shrink. This makes the Great Salt Lake of Utah famous for its shifting boundaries.

IDAHO

WYOMING

Logan
Brigham City
Great Salt Lake

Ogden

Bountiful

Salt Lake City

Tooele
Heber City
Vernal

Orem
Provo
Roosevelt
Utah Lake

NEVADA

UTAH
Duchesne

Nephi
Helper
Price

COLORADO

Delta
Ephraim

Gunnison
Green River

Richfield
ARCHES NATIONAL PARK

Moab

Beaver

Panguitch
Monticello

Cedar City
Blanding

Lake Powell

St. George
Kanab

Virgin River

Lake
Mead

ARIZONA

NEW MEXICO

30. SALTY LAKES

We now know that the Great Salt Lake of Utah is the saltiest on our planet. But have you ever wondered where all this salt comes from? And if all lakes are salty, then what's the deal with freshwater lakes? How do they avoid all the salt? Let's answer a few of these baffling questions.

Let's attempt to answer why water bodies get salty. It's taken for granted that seas and oceans are salty, but how did all that salt get in there in the first place? It is because of the salt that is inherently present in nature, just like the minerals that are strewn all over the world. Oceans are like the dumping grounds of rivers from all over the world. All rivers deposit their salt in the ocean. While the water from these oceans evaporate, the salt is always left behind. This is why, over the span of their existence, oceans have become saltier and saltier.

Now that we've solved the mystery of the salty oceans, let us understand why lakes get salty. In essence, the reason is the same. Salty lakes are also known as terminal lakes. Like oceans, these lakes serve as the dumping grounds of several rivers. While every river is depositing its waters into these lakes, no river originates from the lake and takes water out. This is why the salt in these lakes keeps accumulating and they become salty. On the other hand, freshwater lakes serve as the starting point for different rivers and provide water to them. Along with the water, salt also flows out, lowering the concentration of salts in these lakes.

31. NAMIB DESERT

The Namib Desert in Namibia seems to be going through quite an identity crisis. It can't seem to decide if it is a beach or a desert. It's a desert by the seashore! How does that happen? Shouldn't the sea negate the desert-like atmosphere? This is a case of contradictory climate, and here's the reason.

The first rather strange thing about the climate of the Namib Desert is that it barely ever rains here, yet the air is almost always humid. Confused? Blame the topography of this land. The wet winds that blow from the ocean make the air humid.

Because there are no hills or mountain ranges to block these winds and cause rainfall, they just blow by.

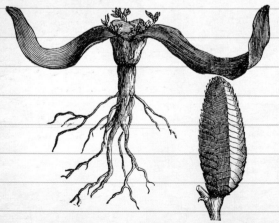

Apart from that, while blowing through the hot Namib Desert, most of the moisture evaporates. This causes the inner edges of the desert to be driest. At the coastal areas, because the winds are laden with moisture, the humidity is high and it gives rise to fog. The temperatures here are between

FAST FACT . . .
The dense fog and strong ocean currents near the coastline of Namib causes ships to lose their way.

58°-67°F during the summers and 46°-57°F during the winters.

Due to such contradictory weather conditions and a surprising topography – where the desert meets the ocean – the coastline of Namib is every photographer's delight.

FAST FACT . . .
The Welwitschia plant is found only in the Namib Desert. This plant is considered to be a living fossil.

32. THE DEAD SEA

Have you ever wondered where this name comes from? What could the sea have possibly done to be called dead? This depressing sea is situated at the border of Jordan. The sea got its name because of the lack of any sort of life in the form of fish or seaweed. It's an empty sea. Here's why.

FAST FACT . . .
It's difficult to drown in the Dead Sea because its high concentration of salts will keep you floating.

The Dead Sea, which is 42 miles long and 11 miles wide, is located in one of the lowest areas on the Earth. Water from all neighboring lakes and rivers empties itself into this sea, making it very salty. The Dead Sea also contains a high content of minerals such as magnesium chloride, calcium chloride, and potassium chloride. This is why it is difficult for life, apart from a few extremophiles to survive in the Dead Sea.

FAST FACT . . .
The Dead Sea is not actually a sea, but a salt lake.

33. STRATOVOLCANOS

The stratovolcano is characterized by its shape, which is conical and steep, like Mount Fuji, which is a stratovolcano. Other volcanoes have gradual slopes. Why do the shapes of various volcanoes differ? The answer to it lies just beneath.

Vulcan – the Roman God of Fire

Mount Fuji is a steep, conical stratovolcano. The lava that erupted from Fuji was viscous. It couldn't travel fast and spread to form a gentle slope. It hardened quickly and formed a steep slope. Other such volcanoes are Mount Mayon in Philippines and Mount Agua in Guatemala. Due to their abruptness and low viscosity, the heights of stratovolcanoes is also high.

Another kind of volcano is the shield volcano, which has a very gradual slope. In these volcanoes, the lava that erupts is low in viscosity, which makes it move faster. It slides down and forms a very gentle slope before hardening. The largest shield volcano is Mauna Lao in the islands of Hawaii. As the lava from such volcanoes flows fast and spreads, their base is very wide.

FAST FACT . . .
The word volcano originates from the name of the Roman God of fire – "Vulcan."

34. 84 DAYS OF SUMMER

The Sun doesn't set for 84 days in Barrow, Alaska. This means that for 84 days in a row, Eskimos don't see any twinkling stars or shining moon. That's because, for 84 days straight, it's always day time! Though it sounds pretty bizarre and unimaginable, it's true.

Barrow, in Alaska, is located near the North Pole of the Earth. In fact, it's the 9th most northern city in the world, and northernmost point in the USA. While most places in the world experience a sequence of night and day every 24 hours, Alaska sees the light of day for just 84 days because of its positioning!

This means that the residents of Alaska have to stock up aluminum foil to stick on their windows every 12 hours so that they can have a good night's sleep, because it won't be naturally dark for 84 days in a row!

Conversely, does this mean that during winter it's constantly pitch dark once the sun does decide to set? Not really. There's a small amount of "civil light" for at least 3 hours during the "dark days."

So the next time you take anything for granted, even something as arbitrary as the

ALASKA

rising and the setting of the Sun or the moon, think about the people residing in Alaska, who sit twiddling their thumbs waiting for the next sunrise or sunset.

FAST FACT . . .

Even the moon stays up continuously for all the "dark days." It just moves from one side of the sky to the other.

35. THE ARIZONA DESERT

The Arizona Desert freezes during the night. Though we're not talking literally, the temperatures do drop quite low. Though it's unimaginable to imagine that a desert is toasted during the day and near freezing temperatures at night, it is indeed possible to see a variation of around 50°F between day and night.

The phenomenon of such a large variation of temperatures in deserts can be attributed to the lack of humidity in arid regions. Humidity is partially responsible for trapping the heat in the environment. So, even though the deserts get quite hot during the day, because of the absence of humidity, all the heat is lost very quickly at night.

FAST FACT . . .

The Arizona Desert is hot enough to evaporate 20 times the amount of rainfall it receives.

This causes a sudden dip in temperature. In Arizona, it dips to 35°F. Now that could make anyone go "Brrr!" right?

FAST FACT . . .

Deserts don't receive rainfall for years on end, but when it does rain in the desert, it is usually destructive and violent.

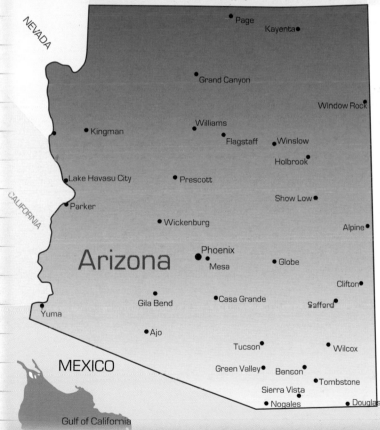

UTAH

COLORADO

NEVADA

• Page

Kayenta•

• Grand Canyon

Window Rock•

• Williams

• Kingman

Flagstaff• •Winslow

Holbrook•

Lake Havasu City• • Prescott

Show Low •

CALIFORNIA

•Parker

• Wickenburg

Alpine •

Arizona

Phoenix •
•Mesa

• Globe

Clifton•

Gila Bend

•Casa Grande

Safford•

•Yuma

• Ajo

Tucson•

Wilcox

MEXICO

Green Valley•

• Wilcox

Benson•

•Tombstone

Sierra Vista•

• Nogales

•Douglas

Gulf of California

NEW MEXICO

36. MOUNT RORAIMA

This tabletop mountain is situated in the Pakaraima mountain chain of South America. Apart from being the tallest mountain in the range, it is two billion years old!

Mount Roraima is 9,219 feet high. It was first discovered by Sir Walter Raleigh in 1596. The Pakaraima mountain range is one of the oldest geological structures on the Earth's surface.

FAST FACT . . .
Table top mountains get formed when a chunk of land starts rising due to pressures from under the Earth's surface. This is exactly how Mount Roraima got formed when continents started drifting apart.

Due to such unique conditions, the environment of Roraima is home to several fascinating species, such as the carnivorous Pitcher plant.

FAST FACT . . .
Unlike the usual mountains, due to the sturdiness of sandstone, the table top mountains didn't fold under pressure. They just kept rising.

What is interesting is that the mountain has been formed out of the rock from the Precambrian Era that dates back to between 4 billion and 540 million years ago.

37. DJIBOUTI

Say hello to an entire country that's sandy and dry all over. This is a country that's located in the north-eastern part of Africa and covers about 8,958 square miles. But almost the entire country is a dry, rocky piece of land.

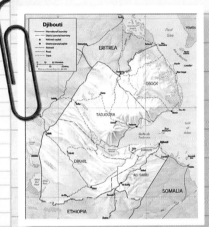

The instability was caused mainly because of the climate, which hardly offers any means of employment to its residents. The total population of this country is 905,564 of which almost 50 percent is unemployed.

Djibouti was founded in 1285 by the Ifat Sultanate. From 1843 to 1886, this arid country was under the rule of the French. After that, the country changed hands from the French to other rulers and finally, in 2000, this country gained political stability.

FAST FACT . . .
The current population of Djibouti is approximately 792,198.

38. TEMPLE OF THE TOOTH

It looks like the tooth-fairy has an official address! The Temple of Tooth in Sri Lanka is actually a Buddhist temple which is dedicated to a canine tooth of Lord Buddha. This temple is situated in a place called Kandy.

The Temple of Tooth was constructed in 1545 in Kandy. Before that, people literally fought tooth and nail for possession of this tooth, because it was believed that whoever was in possession of the tooth, had the right to rule the land. So the tooth gained a position of prime political importance.

Because of the amount of importance attached to it, there were several fraudulent replicas made to gain control over the state.

But where does the legend of the tooth begin from? It begins at the time when Buddha had attained nirvana and his final rites were to be performed. A monk named Khema, who was extremely fond of his master Buddha, slyly snatched a tooth from Buddha's upper canines. It was there that the legend of

the traveling tooth began. It got embellished as it passed from mouth to mouth.

However, if you visit the temple hoping to catch a glimpse of this problematic tooth, you probably won't, because it's stored in a gold casket within which there are six more caskets. The last one, the tiniest little one, is the one that contains the tooth.

FAST FACT . . .

The Temple of Tooth is of prime importance because it is believed that it improves the quality of your karmic cycles once you visit it. And it is a must to visit this tooth temple at least once in a lifetime.

39. NEW ZEALAND

It's a well-known fact that this country shakes and wobbles every once in a while. This rather shaky tendency has caused its residents to name it the "shaky country." But what's causing New Zealand to get on the dance floor and shake every once in a while? Here's what.

New Zealand is an island country situated in the southwestern part of the Pacific Ocean. This country is made up of two great masses of land called the North and South Islands. The total area of New Zealand is about 103,483 square miles. It shakes because it is located above two tectonic plates – the Australian plate and Pacific plate.

When these plates, which are about 62 miles in thickness, collide with each other, it results

FAST FACT . . .
New Zealand was the last big land mass to be populated. Of course, the uninhabitable parts of the Polar Regions are not taken into consideration here.

in earthquakes. Most of these
earthquakes are not of a very
high magnitude, but it's enough
to send a shiver down New
Zealand's spine. On the other
hand, the plates sometimes
float away from each other
and create a certain amount of
elasticity, which also results in
an earthquake.

Sir Edmund Hillary

40. TIMBUKTU

Often, when something gets lost, it is referred to as being "somewhere in Timbuktu." Timbuktu is considered to be a tucked away place in one corner of the world where all missing things go. Few people are actually aware of its existence. But Timbuktu is a real place in Africa. Care to find out why this place has such a negative connotation?

This city was actually founded in the 11th century. However, a lot of the stories about this place stem from the fact that people who visit it often feel like they are visiting the end of the Earth. The narrow dirt tracks melt into the vast Sahara desert. The residents though, are far from "lost" and "remote." They are so rich in culture and history that they are in possession of treasures that could make other countries green with jealousy.

There are several books of hand-tooled goatskin covers that contain many pages of Arabic calligraphy. These treasures are safely hidden in the sand, or in the houses of the residents, safe from the prying eyes of collectors.

It is because of these manuscripts that Timbuktu is considered to be something out of a fairy tale from the past. Approximately 50,000 of these manuscripts still survive, and they are all between 400 and 600 years old. Timbuktu was thriving, with a university and several schools educating its citizens. It was actually considered to be the intellectual center of Africa.

41. NATURAL WONDERS

The seven man-made wonders of the world are pretty famous. Did you know that there are seven natural wonders of the world too? All of them are equally breathtaking. Here's the complete list.

Grand Canyon

This wonder is situated in the northwestern Arizona. It was first discovered by the Spanish in 1540. The Grand Canyon National Park was established much later in 1919. The colorful rocks, which have been eroded by the Colorado River and its tributaries for millions of years, have formed breathtaking patterns.

Aurora Borealis

Also called the Northern Lights, they are formed when the atmospheric particles of the Earth collide with the particles of Sun that have sneaked into the Earth's atmosphere. The dance of such lights in the southern hemisphere is called Aurora Australis.

Mount Everest

The highest mountain on Earth, which is 29,035 feet high, has also made it into this list. It was first scaled by Tenzing Norgay and Edmund Hillary in 1953.

Paricutin

Here's a volcano whose making was witnessed by people. This volcano first erupted in the corn fields of Mexico in 1943 and is now 1,345 feet high.

Victoria Falls

This is the largest curtain of flowing water, and has earned its place in the list of the Seven Wonders of the World. It is situated between Zambia and Zimbabwe and was originally known as Mosi-ao-Tunya. It is 1.25 miles wide and 328 feet deep.

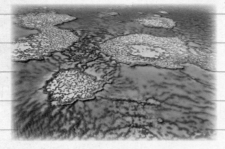

The Great Barrier Reef

This 1,242 miles long reef along Australia's northeastern coastline started forming 300 million years ago. It has been formed by the skeletal remains of the coral polyps.

Ancient Sequoia trees

These are natural wonders that are still growing in California's Sequoia National Park. The trees are about 1800-2700 years old and have grown to the height of 100 feet. They are found on California's Sierra Nevada Mountains at elevations from 5,000-7,000 feet.

42. URAL MOUNTAINS

While most continents are divided by oceans, Europe and Asia are divided by a mountain range – the Ural Mountains. Strangely, the mountain range does not form a very tall divide. The Ural range has plateaus and mountains at low heights.

The Ural Mountains run through western Russia. They are 1,600 miles long and 93 miles wide. The highest peak in this mountain range is Mount Narodnaya, which is around 6,217 feet in height.

These mountains were formed about 300 million years ago by the end of the Carboniferous era. The Ural mountain range started appearing when the tectonic plate of western Siberia collided with the Baltica and North America plates.

The Ural Mountains are rich in mineral deposits, coal, precious, and semi-precious stones. This range forms the mineral base of Russia.

FAST FACT . . .
The Ural mountains stretch from the Arctic Ocean to the Caspian Sea.

43. AUSTRALIA

While most continents are divided into countries, there's one continent that is made up of only one country – Australia – the 6th largest country in the world. But this is only one of the long list of things about Australia that will make your jaw drop.

Australia sprawls across 2,969,907 square miles and has the third largest ocean territory. Even though Australian citizens have the entire continent to themselves, 80 percent of the population stays within 60 miles from the coast. Due to this, Australia has one of the most urbanized coasts in the world.

FAST FACT . . .

The Dingo Fence in Australia was built to keep wild dingos out of South-Eastern Australia. It is called a quirky version of the Great Wall of China because the fence is 3,488 miles long, which is twice as long as the Great Wall of China.

Apart from the peculiar demographics, even the flora and fauna in Australia is unique. Plants, animals, and birds found in Australia are found nowhere in the world. A classic example of this is the kangaroo.

44. TYPES OF MAPS

Were you under the impression that maps are usually political in nature? Apart from always being politically correct, there are several other criteria that the different kinds of maps are required to meet. There are six basic types of maps. Here's how they are categorized.

Maps are important to know exactly where we stand on our large, not quite round Earth. The journey of maps has been a long, exhausting one, and is not over yet!

Maps began their journey on cloth and papyrus with Aristotle, way back in 350 B.C., and continued to evolve till today. We have graduated to electronic GPS devices that map the areas on the go.

Most of us refer to an atlas, which has all the reassuring boundaries and dots for us to look at and understand. If we observe closely, we can see different kinds of maps within that Atlas.

We have **climate maps** that show temperature changes and precipitation patterns.

We have **economic maps** that demarcate regions on the basis of the crops they grow or minerals that are found.

FAST FACT . . .
The art and science of making maps is called "cartography."

Some maps show us the different boundaries of a country, along with their mountains, rivers, lakes, seas, and various other natural landforms of that area. We call these **physical maps**.

Some maps show the different cities, towns, counties, and countries of an area. These maps show political boundaries of a country and demarcate the states within a country. We call them **political maps**.

Some maps show us different routes connecting different places. These are called **road maps**. We need these maps while traveling from one place to another.

Some maps highlight the elevations in a particular area. These are known as **topographical maps**.

Now that we know the different kinds of maps, let's recognize them the next time we browse through an atlas!

OCEAN CURRENT

45. THE ALLUVIAL FAN

An alluvial fan is the name given to a triangular section formed at the mouth of a river. The triangle is usually created when a fast flowing river broadens at the mouth because of the topography of that area. This broadening creates a near-perfect triangle.

FAST FACT . . .

There is also another category called the colluvial fans, which are not caused by water but by landslides.

The sediments that are deposited by the river in this triangle are alluvium, which is made up of small particles of soil, and are very fertile in nature. That's why this part is called the alluvial fan. Usually, alluvial fans are caused by flash floods when the flowing water suddenly causes a swell.

There are also underwater alluvial fans. They are caused by underwater currents formed due to melting glaciers.

FAST FACT . . .

The converging of many alluvial fans is called a "bajada."

46. BAYOU COUNTRY

Bayou is derived from the Chaoctaw word "bayuk," which means a small stream. Bayou represents that part of the river which is very slow moving, almost stationary. Usually, it forms a swamp. Bayous are found in flat areas.

Bayous usually exist as fresh water or salt water bodies. Sometimes they can be both. Bayous are also sites for a varied form of vegetation ranging from moss to tall Cyprus trees. That's why they can provide shelter to various kinds of life forms such as birds, shrimps, and even alligators.

FAST FACT . . .
Bayou Bartholomew, situated in the states of Arkansas and Louisiana, is the largest bayou in the world. It is 375 miles long.

The American Gulf coast is called the Bayou Country.

FAST FACT . . .
A combination of fresh water and salt water bayous is called "brackish waters."

It is home to Cajun and Creole cultures. People have been living in this part of the world for more than thousand years. In places such as these, transportation is usually through the waterways.

47. ATOLLS

The remnants of a sea volcano can be seen in the form of an atoll, which is a ring-shaped coral reef. While this is an interesting structure made by nature, how is it created? Let's find out.

An underwater volcano is called a seamount. For several years, every time a volcano erupted, the lava piled up. With subsequent eruptions, the height of this pile of lava kept increasing and finally reached the surface of the sea. It formed an island. Corals then arrived and started building their homes on this part of the island.

After that, as the years passed by, the sea started eroding the volcanic soil. The island soon disappeared under the surface of the ocean, but the corals remained. They formed a ring-like structure, which was named "atoll."

Atolls are low-lying and are usually hidden by the ocean waves. Ships often get stuck in them, which is how they get stranded or wreaked.

FAST FACT . . .

The Maldives in Indian Ocean and Kiribati in Pacific Ocean are examples of island nations made of atolls.

48. OCEANIA

You probably know about this region, but not by this name! Oceania refers to the region that includes thousands of islands in the South and Central Pacific Ocean. Australia, too, is one of the islands included in Oceania.

Oceania is mostly made up of Australia and New Zealand. It is also divided into continental islands, low islands, and high islands. The continental islands were one big mass of land before the sea level began to rise and tectonic collisions forced chunks of land to move apart. The High Islands were formed due to volcanic eruptions and the deposition of lava. Much like the Ring Of

FAST FACT . . .
There are 110 endemic species of birds in Oceania.

Fire in the South Pacific Ocean, many volcanoes in the High Islands are still active.

The Low Islands have been formed by corals. They barely manage to reach the sea level. Examples of such islands are Micronesia and Polynesia.

A majority of the fauna on these islands is made up of birds, because they can travel easily from one island to another. As you can imagine, it isn't the same case for animals.

FAST FACT . . .

Lizards and bats are the native animals of Oceania.

The animals that live in Oceania migrated here when the water level was low. This was many million years ago. This is why the wildlife of Oceania is different from the rest of the world.

SNOW

JET STREAMS

WEATHER

CUMULONIMBUS

STRATOSPHERE

HURRICANE

IONOSPHERE

AMMONIA

HAIL

XENON

THE ATMOSPHERE

TORNADOES

RAIN

TROPOSPHERE

FRONTS

49. DRY VALLEYS

The Dry Valleys in Antarctica haven't received rainfall for more than a million years. That's a long time, isn't it? Due to such extreme weather conditions, the Dry Valleys have developed rocks which are very peculiarly shaped.

When talking about the driest place on Earth, the Atacama Desert in Peru is usually spoken of first. However, it's the Dry Valleys of Antarctica that take the cake. These valleys, which are situated right in the center of all that snow and ice, are indeed the driest place on Earth.

The Dry Valleys of Antarctica stretch for over 1,900 square miles and are devoid of water in liquid or frozen form. Unlike its surroundings, there is no ice found. In fact, researchers believe that it hasn't rained in these valleys in almost 2 million years. That's quite a dry spell, isn't it?

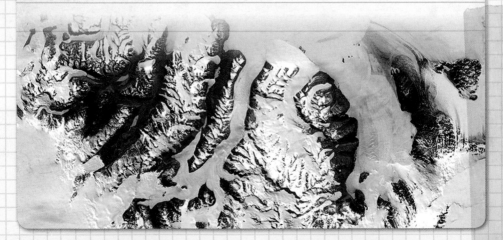

Robert Falcon Scott, a British explorer, who was one of the first to explore the Antarctic, discovered this harsh valley and called it the "Valley of Death" because, according to him, no life form could survive in such an extreme climate.

However, he was quite mistaken. The Dry Valleys support life in the form of lichen, mosses, cyanobacteria, and nematodes.

FAST FACT . . .

Living organisms that can thrive in extreme environments such as that of the Dry Valleys of Antarctica are called extremophiles.

Robert Falcon

50. RAIN

Rain always begins as snow or ice. That means every time you get caught in a rainstorm, you've actually just missed a snowstorm, or a hailstorm! Every rain drop begins its journey as an ice crystal.

You may already know how rain is formed. After all, the process of evaporation and condensation is covered in every textbook. We know that water evaporates, goes up into the atmosphere, forms clouds, and returns to Earth in the form of a million tiny droplets. What we are unaware of, though, is that water doesn't remain in its liquid form throughout

FAST FACT . . .
Rain can fall at a speed
of 17-58 miles per hour.

this process. When water evaporates, it forms a cloud. As more and more droplets evaporate and join it, it forms a larger, darker cloud. The liquid drops now turn into small ice crystals. The reason for this is that it is easier for a cloud to maintain an ice crystal than a wobbly drop of water.

FAST FACT . . .
A rain drop is oval in shape, not the "drop" shape that we draw in our books.

Finally, when the temperature is cool enough, the ice crystal falls and quickly transforms into a drop while rushing down. This is what happens in warmer regions. In colder regions, it maintains its state. In fact, it sometimes grows bigger and falls down in the form of snowflakes or hail stones.

51. TORNADOES IN U.S.A.

America is the recipient of the maximum number of tornadoes in the world. Colloquially known as twisters, more than 1,200 tornadoes occur in the USA annually. In fact, the central strip of this country is even known as Tornado Alley. What about the USA attracts so many tornadoes?

Tornadoes are formed when hot air mixes with cooler air. The cold air from clouds drops very quickly and the warm air keeps rising. That's because cold air is heavy and warm air is light. This alternate upward-downward movement of air causes a spiral movement which forms a shape. When this shape dips down and touches the ground, it is called a tornado.

This funnel-shaped movement of the air is strong enough to lift objects off the ground and carry it up in the air.

Many tornadoes are found in USA because of its topography. Most tornado-prone areas in the Tornado Alley are found in low-lying areas. Due to the low altitude, the air is quite warm while the air high above in the sky is cold. This environment is conducive for tornadoes.

The next time you see a tornado in the distance, take shelter quickly, or you too might reach Oz, like Toto and Dorothy from the Wizard of Oz.

FAST FACT . . .

Tornadoes in the Tornado Alley usually form late in spring or during early fall, when temperature fluctuations are common.

FAST FACT . . .

Thunderstorms called as "supercells" have a higher risk of turning into a tornado.

52. HURRICANES

Hurricanes are like the Zeus of spiral-wind disasters. They are extremely violent, causing a great deal of damage to life, livestock, and property. However, the calmest spot of the hurricane is right in the middle, in the eye of the hurricane!

Hurricanes are formed over moist, warm air that rises up quickly. This usually takes place on the ocean floor. Air from the neighboring areas rushes in and forms the hurricane. However, right in the middle of this hurricane, a tiny part remains very calm.

FAST FACT . . .
Hurricane Katrina, which occurred in 2005, was the third strongest hurricane to make a landfall in the USA.

The wind that is spinning very fast around this eye prevents any high pressure air from entering this area. This is why it remains almost untouched by the violence that the hurricane causes.

53. THE ROCK CYCLE

Did you know that the very Earth we walk on is recycled? You are probably wondering how the ground we walk on can be recycled while we are walking on it. Our planet has a smart trick up its sleeve, which it has been following for billions of years.

This trick is known as rock recycling. Igneous rocks are formed when lava cools down. After a long period of time, the weather changes and other factors cause them to change into sedimentary rocks, like sandstone. When sedimentary rocks get buried deep inside the Earth, they change to become metamorphic rocks. It is just a matter of time before this metamorphic rock melts once again, and spurts out of some unsuspecting volcano as lava.

The Rock Cycle

Igneous Rock — GRANITE

Sedimentary Rock — SANDSTONE

Metamorphic Rock — GNEISS

54. THE TROPOSPHERE

The Earth's atmosphere is divided into four layers. Each layer has a different function. These four layers work as a blanket to cover the Earth and protect it from meteorites and other harmful particles in space.

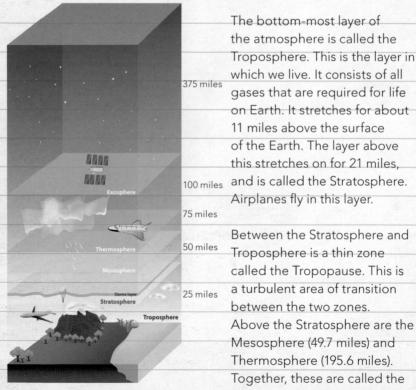

Layers of the atmosphere

375 miles

Exosphere

100 miles

75 miles

Thermosphere

50 miles

Mesosphere

Ozone layer

Stratosphere

25 miles

Troposphere

The bottom-most layer of the atmosphere is called the Troposphere. This is the layer in which we live. It consists of all gases that are required for life on Earth. It stretches for about 11 miles above the surface of the Earth. The layer above this stretches on for 21 miles, and is called the Stratosphere. Airplanes fly in this layer.

Between the Stratosphere and Troposphere is a thin zone called the Tropopause. This is a turbulent area of transition between the two zones. Above the Stratosphere are the Mesosphere (49.7 miles) and Thermosphere (195.6 miles). Together, these are called the

Ionosphere. These layers are responsible for protecting us from the ionized, or electrically charged particles of outer space. All the ions get trapped in this layer.

These ions are also responsible for satellite transmissions. This means that radio, television, etc., all function because of the presence of these particles.

FAST FACT . . .

Our atmosphere is made up of 78 percent nitrogen, 21 percent oxygen, 1 percent argon and carbon, and traces of krypton, neon, xenon, helium, nitrous oxide, methane, and carbon monoxide.

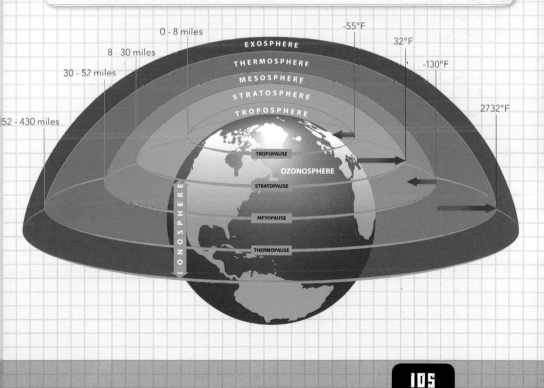

0 - 8 miles

8 - 30 miles

30 - 52 miles

52 - 430 miles

-55°F

32°F

-130°F

2732°F

EXOSPHERE

THERMOSPHERE

MESOSPHERE

STRATOSPHERE

TROPOSPHERE

TROPOPAUSE

OZONOSPHERE

STRATOPAUSE

MESOPAUSE

THERMOPAUSE

IONOSPHERE

55. TYPES OF CLOUDS

Have you ever looked up at the clouds and tried to figure out what shape they resemble?
If you have looked carefully, then you may have noticed that not all clouds are exactly the same. Some are white and fluffy, others are dark and thunderous, while some are just wisps – almost non-existent.

Clouds are made up of very tiny drops of water or ice crystals, depending on the temperature at which they are.

There are four basic types of clouds that can be found in the environment.

Cumulus clouds – These are white, puffy clouds that are piled on top of each other. Even though they are found at the height of 6,000 feet, they pile up and reach great heights and thickness.

FAST FACT . . .
Fog is a stratus kind of a cloud that's found very close to the ground.

Stratus clouds – These are what we call rain clouds. They form rain in warm temperatures and snow in colder regions. They are found at a height of 6,500 feet and are known as low clouds.

Cirrus clouds – These are the thin, wispy clouds that are found high up in the sky. They are found at an altitude of 18,000 feet.

Nimbus clouds – These are cloud which are already raining. They are low clouds, but they do not have a clear base. They usually pair up with the cumulus clouds and form really large clouds. The Cumulonimbus is the largest of such clouds.

FAST FACT . . .
Clouds on Jupiter and Saturn are made of ammonia.

56. JET STREAMS

Jet streams are strong and chilling winds that are found only at very high altitudes. They often pose a problem for many mountaineers. Once the winds begin to blow, mountaineers have no other choice but to retreat to their camp.

Jet streams are found in places where the temperature differences are very high. It usually occurs at very high altitudes. Certain sections of the Earth's surface heat up because of the Sun's rays, while others remain cool. This happens because the surface of the Earth gets unevenly heated by the Sun.

The air above the hot land also heats up and becomes light. This light air begins to rise up.

On the other hand, the cool air, which is heavier, begins to push down and takes the place of the warm air. This causes some swift currents. Jet streams are the names given to such air currents in the Tropopause.

Jet streams usually travel between 80 and 140 miles per hour, though sometimes they can even go to 275 miles per hour, depending on the climate.

FAST FACT . . .
Tropopause is the zone that separates the turbulent troposphere from the cold and calm stratosphere.

FAST FACT . . .
Pilots try not to fly against jet streams because of its strength. They either fly with it or above it.

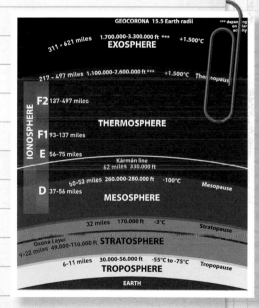

57. FRONTS

While the sky is usually a continuum of blue with various hues into each other, sometimes there is a clear distinction between the two types of air in the sky. This clear line is called a Front. Two types of fronts exist in the atmosphere – the cold front and the warm front.

A front is a zone that is 20 to 100 miles wide. The clashing of fronts can result in rain, storms or windy days. What determines whether the front will be a warm or a cold one? A warm front gets created at the tail ends of precipitation, such as fog. It is found in places where the temperature is warm and the atmosphere has a high pressure. Such conditions usually indicate that the weather is calm.

A warm front usually travels from north to south. It is also less dense than the cold front. This is because of its temperature, which makes the air molecules light and airy.

The cold front, on the other hand is very dense due to its temperature. It's these cold fronts that could be responsible for bringing in extreme weather, like thunderstorms. The cold front travels from west to east. It forms in a low-pressure area where the weather is not stable.

The next time you are caught in a thunderstorm without an umbrella, you know which front to blame!

FAST FACT . . .
Cold fronts are denoted by blue lines with sharp teeth and warm fronts are denoted by red lines with round bumps on a weather map.

FAST FACT . . .
It's always easier to locate a cold front because it's very dense.

997

977

L 982

L 990

L 969

H 1029

58. XENON

Xenon is supposed to be present in our atmosphere in trace amounts. Even though we do not really depend on this gas for survival, scientists have stumbled upon a finding that has left them disturbed – Xenon is missing from the atmosphere. Where did this gas go?

When scientists first discovered that Xenon is missing, many researchers believed that perhaps this gas was merely hiding somewhere in the atmosphere – it had attached itself to another mineral. But probes revealed that it wasn't so. Xenon was a noble gas, and it couldn't attach itself easily to other minerals or compounds in the atmosphere.

Scientists then came up with the theory that perhaps 4 billion years ago, when the Earth's crust was molten, many meteorites rained into the atmosphere, and Xenon escaped into space because it couldn't attach itself to any mineral.

In any case, the hunt is still on, for Mr Xenon.

54

Xe

131.29

Xenon

Date of Discovery: 1898
Discoverer: Sir William Ramsay
Name Origin: From the Greek word xenon (stranger)
Uses: powerful lamps, bubble chambers
Obtained From: liquid air

59. BUTTERFLY-EFFECT

The weather on Earth is dynamic. With the present condition that has global warming threats lurking just around the corner, people make it a point to listen to the weather forecasts carefully. Even so, certain errors creep up.

Weather forecasters have a very responsible job. They predict the weather conditions of a place and inform or alert everyone accordingly. Weather forecasts are especially helpful for fishermen who brave the sea everyday to catch fish. You wouldn't want to get stuck in a hurricane when you're out fishing, would you?

FAST FACT . . .
A corollary to the butterfly-effect is the fact that even small actions can result in major changes.

And so, a slightest misjudgment on the part of the forecaster could cost people their lives. This kind of an error is denoted by the butterfly effect. According to this theory, if a butterfly flaps its wings somewhere in China, it could produce a tornado in Kansas. Of course, that's not to be believed literally. It only means that overlooking a trivial detail can lead to a big error.

60. CLIMATE AND WEATHER

Have you ever wondered about the difference between the weather and the climate? The question has plagued many and left them scratching their heads. It's finally time to put that dilemma to rest.

Weather is a very short-term phenomenon. It points to the environmental circumstances at present, or in the next few hours. Climate, on the other hand, is a long-term phenomenon. It tells you about the nature of a place. That's the reason why we have weather-forecasters, because the weather keeps changing. The climate, on the other hand, remains constant for a long period of time and doesn't really require forecasting.

The climate of a region is determined by taking into consideration the atmosphere, hydrosphere, cryosphere, land surface, and biosphere. To study the weather, you need to focus on day-to-day changes in temperature and precipitation.

FAST FACT . . .

The study of climate is called climatology, but the study of weather is called meteorology.

FAST FACT . . .
The largest snowfall ever recorded in a one year period was 1,224 inches in Mount Rainier, Washington State, United States, between February 19, 1971 and February 18, 1972.

FAST FACT . . .
The highest temperature ever recorded in Antarctica is 159°F, recorded on January 5, 1974.

LIGHTNING

NORTHERN LIGHTS

RAINBOW

TIDE

ICEBERGS

SNOW BLINDNESS

THUNDER

VITAMIN B12

RAIN

NATURAL PHENOMENA

QUICK SAND

DOME ICEBERG

PINNACLE SHAPED

61. NORTHERN LIGHTS IN SPACE

Northern lights are a breathtaking phenomenon. On Earth, it can be witnessed above the magnetic poles in the northern and southern hemispheres. In the northern hemisphere they are called Aurora Borealis and in the southern hemisphere they are called Aurora Australis. However, Earth is not the only planet fortunate enough to view this spectacle.

The dance of the Northern Lights takes place when gaseous particles in the Earth's atmosphere collide with charged up particles from the Sun's atmosphere. What causes these charged up particles to escape from the Sun and enter the Earth's atmosphere? Certain charged particles (electrons and protons) escape the Sun's magnetic field and are blown towards the Earth. Usually, such particles are deflected by the Earth's magnetic field. The magnetic fields above the poles are a little weak, and so these particles are able to sneak in.

FAST FACT . . .
Scientists have discovered that the aural display occurs every 11 years. It last took place in 2013, and will take place next in 2024.

Once inside the Earth's atmosphere, these charged particles collide with particles in the Earth's atmosphere and result in a display of colors. The best seats for this show are along the northwestern part of Canada, northwestern territories of Alaska, southern tip of Greenland and Iceland, northern coast of Norway and coastal waters to the north of Siberia. In the southern hemisphere, they are concentrated around Antarctica and to the south of the Indian Ocean.

FAST FACT . . .

According to the belief of the Inuit in Alaska, the aural lights denote the spirits of animals – seals, salmons, deer, and beluga whales that they hunted.

62. SNOW-BLINDNESS

Can snow really harm your eyes? Yes, it can!
Read on to find out what could go wrong when
you step out on a snowy day to build
a snowman.

The white fluffy snow that we use to make a snowman can also be harmful for us. This pristine snow can act as a mirror and reflect the rays of sunlight. If it was just the sunlight, it wouldn't really be harmful. But the sunlight also carries UV rays (not the cancerous ones) that pose as a big threat to our eyes.

If our eyes are constantly exposed to UV rays, they tend to burn the corners of our cornea. This can make our eyes water. They can also make our eyes appear bloodshot and feel itchy, which is the feeling we get when a grain of sand gets stuck in our eye.

Snow-blindness could cause temporary or permanent loss

FAST FACT . . .

If you do get blinded by the snow, you could try spending a long time in the dark to rest your eyes without rubbing them.

of vision. But all this only happens if we forget to wear the necessary eye protection that we need while stepping out on a snowy day. Make sure you cover those eyes when you step out!

63. LIGHTNING

70 percent of lightning strikes in the Tropics. If you're somewhere in the Tropics you have a better chance of witnessing a spectacular lightning than if you were somewhere else. Why are the Tropics so lightning prone, though?

Lightning occurs when ice crystals inside a cloud move violently, rubbing against each other and creating a large amount of charge that's unbalanced. The charge that gets created is similar to the static electricity that you can create by simply rubbing a piece of wool against a doorknob on a cold, winter morning. You might even see a spark fly!

FAST FACT . . .

Florida is the place where maximum thunderstorms occur. It is, therefore, also a place for maximum lightning.

This rubbing of particles could take place within one cloud, two different clouds or between the cloud and the Earth's surface. In all these cases, lightning is produced.

So where does the most lightning occur? In the year 2001, NASA studied the lightning patterns on Earth from outer space with the help of the Optical Transient Detector and the Lightning Image Censor. This data told them that the Tropics attract the most amount of lightning.

Why so? Simply because the Tropics have the most disturbances in air due to the wind flow from the seas and the oceans. Also, the mountainous terrain of the Tropics makes it a favorite spot for lightning to strike.

FAST FACT . . .
Lightning usually stays off the water. There are very few recorded instances of lightning striking in seas and oceans.

64. LIGHTNING AND THUNDER

The next time you're huddled up indoors watching a thunderstorm, try to notice whether you can see lightning first, or hear the thunder. The startling bolt of lightning will always occur a few seconds before the sky starts rumbling and you hear the loud clap of the thunder.

Have you ever wondered why this could be? The simple reason behind this is that light travels faster than sound. This is why you "see" first and "hear" later.

Sound travels at a speed of 750 miles per hour, but light travels at 186,000 miles an hour. Now that's a huge difference, isn't it?

When the particles in the sky get so charged up and heated while rubbing against each other, they produce a flash of light. You can see the light instantly because of the speed at which light travels. However, you hear the sound a few seconds later because it is considerably slower.

Some fighter planes can fly faster than the speed of sound. Technically, you can see these planes before you hear them. These are called "supersonic" planes.

FAST FACT . . .

To know how far away the lightning occurred, count the number of seconds that elapsed between the lightning and the thunder and divide it by five. This will give you the distance in miles.

65. VITAMIN B12

While everyone is going berserk buying expensive Vitamin B12 supplements, very few are aware that this vitamin is present in our rainwater itself. The next time it rains, you can stand out to get your dose of Vitamin B12 – but be careful, because along with the vitamin, you could also catch a cold!

While the vegans and the non-vegetarians continue to argue about whose diet contains more Vitamin B12, new research has pointed out that rainwater probably contains a certain amount of this elusive vitamin.

Vitamin B12 is a water soluble vitamin. Researchers observed that it was present in perceptible amounts in ponds and seas. When water from these water bodies evaporates and forms clouds, unlike salt, which stays behind, Vitamin B12 goes up along with it. This is why, when the same water is recycled and comes pouring down on our umbrellas, it contains this sneaky vitamin.

This does seem like a boon to those who fret over what they should and shouldn't eat to get their share of this elusive vitamin. But hold your horses, and put your umbrellas down before you go running out open-mouthed to gulp down all the rainwater, because apart from this healthy vitamin, rainwater also brings considerable amounts of dust and pollutants with it. You wouldn't want to drink that, would you?

FAST FACT . . .

A deficiency in Vitamin B12 leads to problems in balance and memory. It can also cause depression, confusion, and soreness of mouth amongst other symptoms.

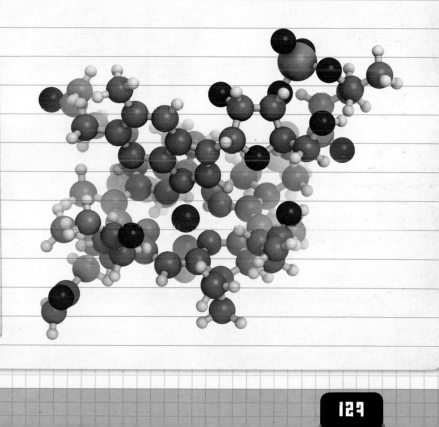

66. THE OCEAN'S MOVEMENT

On beaches, it always seems as if the water is moving forward, toward us, or backward, away from us – depending on the tide. In reality, this is not the case.

Waves are caused when air molecules collide with water molecules. This causes a friction between the two, and energy is transferred from one to another. In reality, the surface of the ocean is rising and falling, not really moving forward or backward.

FAST FACT . . .

Tides are the periodic rise and fall of huge volumes of water due to the gravitational pull of the moon. On the other hand, waves are just the movement of the ocean surface caused by the wind.

In case you're skeptical and want a practical way to test this, observe any object floating in the sea. It only bobs up and down in its place. It does not surge forward with every wave.

Waves from different parts of the ocean sometimes collide. This collision gives rise to a larger wave, known as a rogue wave. Most waves in the oceans are formed because of the wind. However, sometimes, disturbances in the sea bed, such as underwater earthquakes or volcanoes, can also give rise to waves. These waves are a lot more destructive than normal waves. Tsunamis are one example of such a wave that is caused by underwater volcanic eruptions.

FAST FACT . . .
The tidal troughs change every 12 hours according to the position of the moon. Therefore, we have high tide for half the day, and low tide for the other half.

FAST FACT . . .
The raised part of the wave is called the crest, and the depression is called the trough.

67. RAINBOWS

Though rainbows look like an arc in the sky, they are actually only a part of a larger circle! We can't see the circle because the rest of the circle gets obstructed by the horizon. Actually, if seen from an appropriate height, a rainbow is always seen as a full circle.

Rainbows add a pleasant dash of color to the otherwise gray and gloomy rainy days, don't they? You've probably heard stories about the huge pot of gold at the bottom of the rainbow. We regret to inform you that it's not true, but we will tell you what exactly goes into making this colored arc.

Sunlight is actually a range of colors – violet, indigo, blue, green, yellow, orange, and red –

combined into one. When sunlight enters a rain drop at a particular angle, it breaks up into these seven colors.

This splitting of the sunlight into its seven component colors is what we see as our rainbows.

The ingredients that go into the making of a rainbow are a slight drizzle, sunlight, and the correct angle. If sunlight passes through a droplet at a particular angle, the result will always be a rainbow. The lower the Sun is in the sky, the higher the arc of the rainbow will be.

FAST FACT . . .

There's also a phenomenon called as an upside-down rainbow where the Sun shines through ice crystals high in the sky.

FAST FACT . . .

Pilots and mountaineers are sometimes able to see the full circle of the rainbow because they are at a greater height.

68. QUICKSAND

You can actually float on quicksand. Going by numerous Hollywood movies, this statement is blasphemy. In spite of the number of Hollywood characters that have lost their lives to this ravenous monster, it is a fact that it is possible to float on quicksand.

Quicksand is made up of four ingredients – sand, water, clay, and salt. The water loosely fills in the gaps between sand, and is loosely held together by clay. When quicksand is disturbed, the sand particles separate and sink to the bottom. The salt makes the clay particles stick together and they, too, sink to the bottom. This leaves all the liquid on top, which is what makes you get stuck.

But quicksand isn't really as hideous as it's made out to be, because it's usually quite shallow. Even if it weren't, if you remain still, your body will automatically start floating on quicksand.

FAST FACT . . .
Silt is easier to liquefy than sand, which makes it easier to sink in quick-silt than quicksand.

FRST FRCT . . .
Quicksand is most likely to occur in riverbanks, beaches, lake shorelines, marshes and near underground springs.

FRST FRCT . . .
It's true that struggling in quicksand – or just about any quick movement – causes you to sink more. Slow movements are much more effective.

69. ICEBERGS

An iceberg caused the Titanic to sink. This is the extent of most people's knowledge on the subject. Very few people are aware that there are actually more than half a dozen different types of icebergs. Icebergs are large chunks of ice that float on water bodies. They are huge, and are the largest source of most fresh water on Earth.

Icebergs are large blocks of ice that break away from a glacier and begin to float freely. While these frozen floating mountains seem massive, in reality, 90 percent of the iceberg is actually below the surface of the water. You can imagine how large the entire iceberg actually is! That's why the term "tip of the iceberg" is often used to describe just the tiny, visible

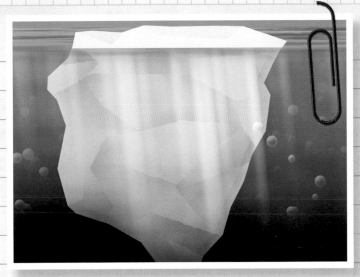

A blocky iceberg

portion of a much bigger object. There are around six types of icebergs – tabular, dome, blocky, wedge, dry-dock, and pinnacle shaped.

The tabular iceberg is a horizontal sheet that has steep sides. The ice keeps accumulating on top of it as time goes by.

The dome shape one is round at the edges.

The blocky iceberg has a flat top and resembles a block of ice.

The wedge is an iceberg with a pointed top, somewhat like that of a pyramid.

A dry-dock is one that makes rough U-shape

A pinnacle consists of one or more pointed edges.

FAST FACT . . .
Icebergs are 100 percent fresh water.

FAST FACT . . .
The Arctic icebergs are made of ice that's more than 3000 years old.

EARTHQUAKE

AVALANCHE

FLOOD

WILD FIRE

ANTARCTICA

CONTINENTAL DIVIDE

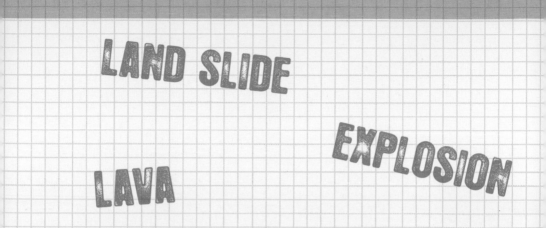

LAND SLIDE

EXPLOSION

LAVA

NATURAL DISASTERS

TSUNAMI

HURRICANE

CRYOVOLCANO

70. YELLOWSTONE NATIONAL PARK

This national park, situated in Wyoming, USA is famous for its hot springs and exploding geysers. Let's take a peek at what lies beneath the Yellowstone National Park to see what makes it so famous. We promise you, the view makes it worth the while.

The story that made the Yellowstone National Park what it is today took place around 640,000 years ago. Of course, none of us were around at that time to witness and applaud the magnificent show that nature had put up. Nevertheless, the explosion played an important role in sculpting the Yellowstone National Park of today's era.

This national park is situated on a very weak zone. This zone has cracks in the crust of the Earth called the Continental Divide. 640,000 years ago lava seeped up from the crack, causing an explosion that formed a 45 by 30-miles crater. Today, this crater, filled with water, is located right in the center of the park.

Because of the unstable zone on which Yellowstone is located, it experiences close to 2,000 earthquakes and is dotted with a number of hot springs and geysers. They keep reminding us that another explosion, just like the one that took place years ago, might be on its way soon.

FAST FACT . . .
Five percent of the Yellowstone National Park is covered with water, 15 percent with grass, and the remaining 80 percent is under the canopy of forest.

FAST FACT . . .
The Yellowstone National Park was America's first national park, to be established in 1872.

71. VOLCANO IN ANTARCTICA

It seems a little off to imagine a mountain spewing fire in the middle of all the ice that covers the Southern Pole of Earth. What we find so odd today was actually quite a common occurrence a long time ago.

FAST FACT . . .

Volcanic eruptions send a blast of greenhouse gases (primarily CO_2) into the atmosphere. This causes the atmosphere to heat up.

This fascinating fact came to light when it was revealed on a website in 2008 by Hugh F.J. Corr and David G. Vaughan. They found a layer of ash buried underneath 23 centuries of snowfall. On studying the depth of this ashen layer, the scientists concluded that the eruption took place in 325 B.C., around the time when

Alexander the Great was creating his empire.

Geologists also say that this explosion is probably similar to the one that took place in Iceland in 2004, when the ash was blown seven miles into the air.

FAST FACT . . .
A kind of volcano that emits water, ammonia, and methane instead of molten rock is known as Cryovolcano.

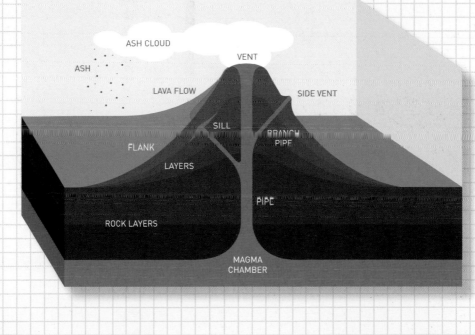

ASH CLOUD

VENT

ASH

LAVA FLOW

SIDE VENT

SILL

BRANCH PIPE

FLANK

LAYERS

PIPE

ROCK LAYERS

MAGMA CHAMBER

72. AVALANCHES

An avalanche is like a landslide, but in snow. To be rescued from an avalanche is extremely difficult, because of the huge amounts of snow involved. How are avalanches caused?

An avalanche usually occurs 24 hours after a snowstorm. This is because of the thick blanket of snow that settles on the slope. An avalanche begins with little powdery snow that begins hurtling down the slope. As it slides down, it collects more snow along the way, and finally becomes a catastrophic disaster.

Factors that affect the magnitude of the avalanche are temperature, storminess, steepness of the slope, and the direction of the avalanche.

After the avalanche ends, the snow that had slid down hardens like concrete. This makes rescue operations particularly difficult. The chances of a person getting rescued 45 minutes after being stuck in an avalanche are very dim.

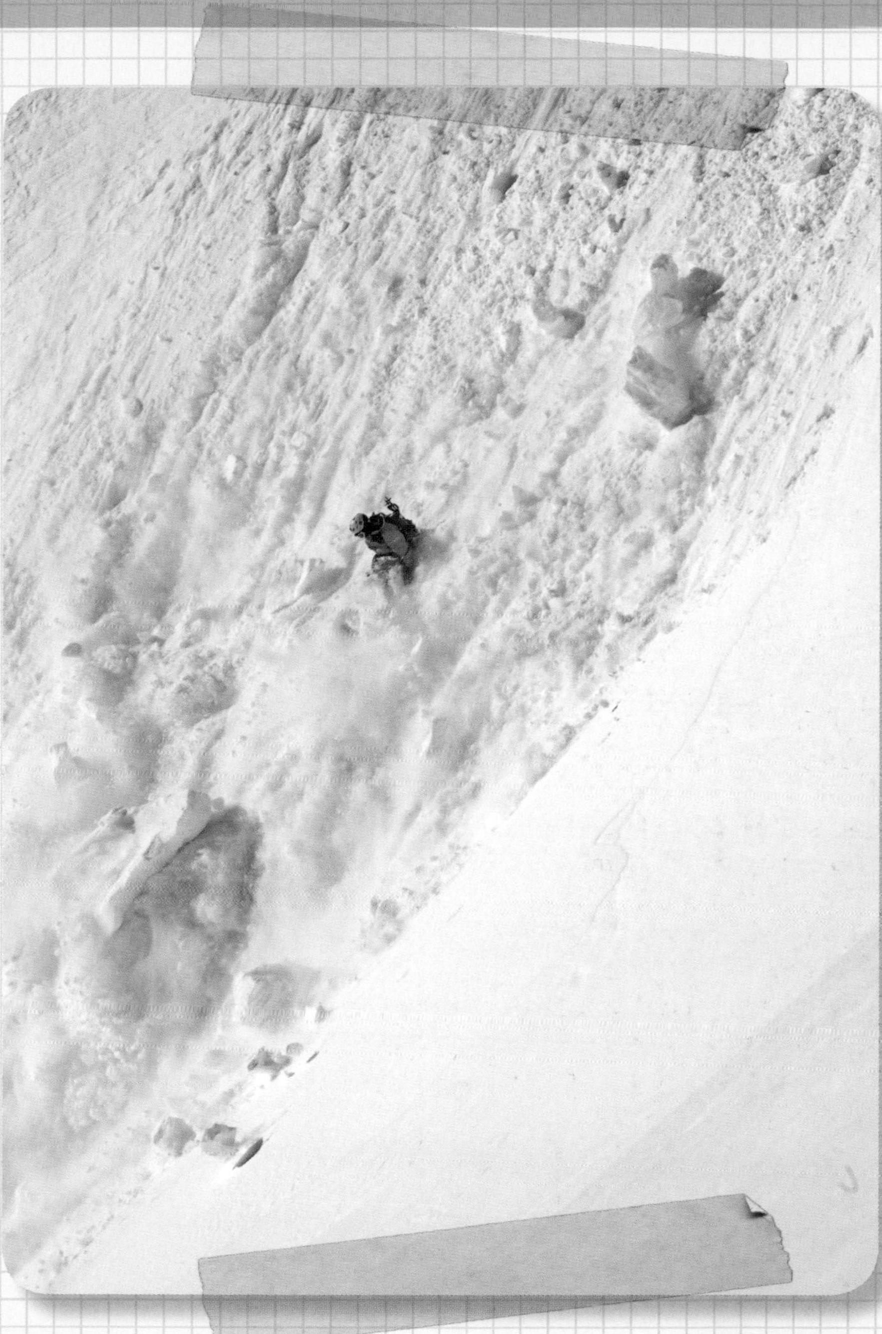

73. FLOODS

Lately, the entire world seems to be flooded with problems, the increasing number of floods being one of them. Several scientists are trying to find out what could be causing these. Here's a peep at what the reasons could be.

Floods are caused due to several reasons, the most common factor being rivers or streams that overflow their banks. Floods like these are quite common and most people get enough warning time to evacuate and reach a safer place.

Coastal flooding takes place when a storm or tsunami causes the sea to rise and surge inland.

However, there are certain floods which are of catastrophic proportions. These floods are believed to take place only once every 100 years. However, this means that there is a 1 percent chance of these floods taking place in any year.

Of late, scientists believe that the frequency of these floods have increased. There are several possible reasons for this increase. Scientists believe that floods of such catastrophic proportions take place only

FAST FACT . . .

The top five deadliest floods in world history occurred when the Huang He (Yellow) River in China exceeded its banks.
The yellow silt in the river can pile up higher than the land around it, causing the water to spill out of its causeway and onto the flat land surrounding it.

once in 100 years. They have isolated several possible causes, such as excessive rainfall, damaged dams, and the melting polar caps. Apart from causing obvious damage to life, livestock, and property, such floods also strip fertile lands of its nutrients. It has been suggested that the reason could be the rapidly changing climate due to global warming. That's one of the prime reasons why polar caps are melting.

74. WILD FIRES

Wild fires are another example of natural disasters that cause a lot of damage to life and property. The USA witnesses around 100,000 wild fires every year, which destroy around 4-5 million acres of land.

Wild fires usually take place in areas with extremely dry weather. Areas with a lot of sun-dried vegetation and open places are susceptible to wild fires. In USA, the hot spots for wild fire are Montana, Idaho, Wyoming, Washington, Colorado, Oregon, and California.

Wild fires can be caused by a number of factors, including lightning, volcanic eruptions or even just the Sun's heat. Once a wildfire starts, it can spread at the rate of 14.29 miles per hour.

FAST FACT . . .

One of the most dangerous aspects of such fires are the convection currents in the air, which can produce major fire storms and tornadoes. These can throw embers and other burning objects beyond the main fire, causing spot fires that in turn can start new fires in other directions.

Even though wild fires are very destructive in nature, there's a silver lining to this rather destructive cloud. Wild fires help agriculture by returning nutrients back to the soil. They also serve as disinfectants and help to sanitize the wild.

FAST FACT . . .

Four out of five wild fires are triggered by humans. Nature only plays the role of enhancing the proportions.

PIRANHA

SARGASSO

BULLFROG

DINOSAURS

DINOSAURS

PINUS LONGAEVA

CHAMELEON

ANGLER FISH

LEATHERBACK TURTLES

MADAGASCAR

LIFE AROUND US

VATICAN CITY

NO-FLY ZONES

PLANKTON

75. NORTHERN HEMISPHERE

The Earth is equally divided by the Equator into two halves. However, most of its people live in the Northern Hemisphere. This might seem like a strange coincidence, but there are a number of factors that contribute to this.

The explanation for why more people live in the Northern Hemisphere than the Southern is actually quite simple. 90 percent of the Northern Hemisphere is made up of land, while 90 percent of the Southern Hemisphere is made up of water. We know that man cannot live in water. Hence, most people live in the Northern Hemisphere.

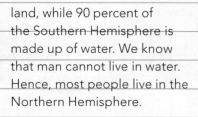

Another theory says that fewer people migrated to the Southern Hemisphere as the lands in that part of the Earth were separated by oceans. Since technology was not as advanced then as it is now, people had no means to travel across the ocean back then. The most populated city in the world, Tokyo, Japan, is situated in the Northern Hemisphere. Even if we carefully observe other populated cities such as Manhattan, New York, and Mumbai, they are situated in the Northern Hemisphere. This is usually because of the favorable climatic conditions. On the other hand, the vast glacial lands of Antarctica, that sprawl across a significant part of the Southern Hemisphere, are uninhabited by humans. These are some of the reasons that contribute to the higher population in the Northern Hemisphere.

FAST FACT . . .
The area 20–40 degrees north of the Equator, where most people thrive, is called the "sweet spot."

76. NO-FLY ZONES

There are certain places over which it is illegal to fly a plane. One such place is the Buckingham Palace. You will probably never see this palace from a bird's view; that is if you're traveling in an airplane. That's because the government of the UK has slotted the area above the Buckingham Palace as a no-fly zone.

This brings us to what no-fly zones are, and why they are enforced. No-fly zones were invented for security purposes. The story of these zones began somewhere around the First World War, when countries began to develop their own aircraft with the intention of attacking other countries.

In this scenario, it was decided that a certain amount of control over the skies of sensitive areas would bring a lot more security and order to the war. Hence, many no-fly zones were introduced. The United Nations is required to authorize the no-fly zones proposed by any country.

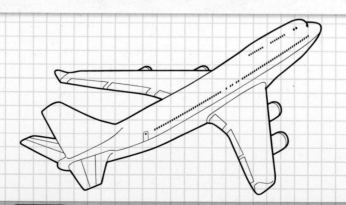

FAST FACT . . .

A no-fly zone was imposed over Libya in 2011 by UN in response to the violence orchestrated by Muammar Gaddafi.

Therefore, we have no-fly zones over monuments such as the Buckingham Palace and the Taj Mahal. No-fly zones had also been imposed by the UN over sensitive regions, such as those where Kurdish populations reside, to save defenseless and innocent people from Saddam Hussein's attack.

77. VATICAN CITY

People living in the Vatican City (which is actually a country) don't have an address! Imagine living in a country so small that there's no need for a street address! The Vatican City is the smallest country in the world. It is enclosed within a wall. Let's know more about it.

But a peculiar thing about this country, apart from its size, is that none of the residents are permanent residents.
This country houses only those people who work at the Vatican. Once they stop working, their citizenship is revoked. There's a

The story of the Vatican City dates back to 1929 when it was formed by the Lateran Treaty. Since then, it has been ruled by the Pope. It is 0.17 square miles in area—that's roughly the size of a golf course—and houses a population of around 750 people.

FAST FACT . . .
While Latin is considered to be a dead language, the ATMs in Vatican City are the only ones that use Latin.

lot more at stake than just your job when you're working there! Vatican City is enclosed in a wall inside Rome, in Italy. Because of its size, it doesn't require a street address as all houses are located a few yards away from the post office. Perhaps that's why its citizens send out more mails than anyone else on the planet.

It has been observed that on an average, a Vatican citizen sends about 7,200 mails a year.

78. DINOSAURS

We've watched in awe as these large reptiles roar and stomp about in a mad rage in movies, but the fact that they belonged to the Cretaceous period isn't so well-known. The large creatures vanished along with this period.

The Cretaceous period is the span of geological time that dates back to 145–65 million years ago. During this time, one big mass of land called Pangaea was beginning to break up, and the continents were starting to drift apart.

This was the time when dinosaurs ruled the land. While there were mammals during that era too, they were smaller in size than these large egg-laying lizards. Earth in the Cretaceous period was witnessing many earthquakes and volcanoes. Because of such explosions, huge amounts of CO_2 escaped into the atmosphere. This CO_2 formed a kind of warm blanket around the Earth's surface by trapping all the heat in the atmosphere. Due to the growing temperatures, the dinosaurs preferred to stay close to the Poles where the climate was cooler. So it seems like global warming has been around for quite a while! Towards the end of the Cretaceous period, some 65 million years ago, a meteor crashed into the Earth's surface and caused mass destruction. The dinosaurs disappeared due to the impact and along with that, this period came to an end.

FAST FACT . . .
The intelligence of a dinosaur is calculated by comparing the size of its body to the size of its brain. It's called the "encephalization quotient."

79. SPIDERS

If you think spiders are icky creatures and even the thought of them crawling up your arms gives you goosebumps, this fact might freak you out. Our Earth is infested with these eight-legged creepy crawlies. There are an estimated 50,000 spiders per acre of green land! As Ron (of Harry Potter fame) once said, "Why spiders? Why couldn't it be butterflies?"

While most are found on land and even in the driest of areas, some have made the edges of lakes and ponds their home. While many spiders can live a longer life in captivity than they live in the wild, the larger spiders tend to get a tad aggressive in confined spaces.

The reason there are so many spiders on Earth is because these resilient creatures can survive in almost any kind of climate. In fact, Antarctica is the only spider-free zone in the world. Spiders can live on trees, plants, grass blades, in your backyard, just anywhere.

FAST FACT . . .

A snow-spider is a rare spider in Eastern Africa. It is completely white in color and spins a black web.

FAST FACT . . .

The largest spider observed by scientists was 8 feet long and weighed 530 pounds. Its legs were broken because it couldn't carry its own weight.

So they attack when they are touched because of their heightened senses.

FAST FACT . . .

There's a collection of holy spiders in China that were hatched roughly 2800 years ago. It is said that these spiders do not die of natural causes and so they are believed to have been living since the existence of the Mang-Tsun dynasty.

80. THE OLDEST TREE

The oldest tree on Earth has been found in the White Mountains of California. Can you guess how old this tree is? 5062 years old! Another absurd part about it is that it hasn't been named yet.

could date its core. Finally, Tom Harlan at the Laboratory of Tree-Ring Research recognized the core to be 5062 years old. Other old trees include Methuselh, also located in the White Mountains of California. It is about 1350 years old. Another one is the Zoroastrian Sarv, a Mediterranean Cyprus, which is 4000 years old. It is located in Iran.

The oldest tree on Earth is of the Pinus longaeva species. It was discovered by a man in the 1950s, who died before he

FAST FACT . . .
One method to determine the age of a tree is by counting the concentric rings in its trunk.

81. MARTIALISHEUREKA ANT

Many peculiar species are found under the canopy of trees in the Amazon rainforest, but a species of ant, called Martialisheureka, takes the cake and nibbles on it too! For starters, this species of ant is around 120 million years old.

Martialisheureka is a species of ant that is 0.07-0.11 inches in length. This pale-colored ant is also blind. Martialisheureka means "ant from Mars." The name is justified, because it displays characteristics that are not found anywhere on the Earth's surface. Scientists, on further research, have found out that this particular ant has evolved from the wasp. This ant has large mandibles, which it uses for catching its prey.

As this species of ant is blind, scientists have also formed the theory that perhaps this ant is an ancestor of the sub-terranean blind species.

FAST FACT . . .
The habitat of Martialisheureka is hidden in the soil, which lessens its competition with other ants and reduces the instances of conflict.

FAST FACT . . .
Mandibles are present in the anterior portion on the ant's bodies. They serve as the ant's jaws. Ants can break, chew, or hold their food with the help of these mandibles.

82. PIRANHAS

Piranhas are one of the most dangerous species of fish that live on Earth. These little fish are quick and lethal. They eat up their prey in a matter of a few seconds, before the prey even realizes it's being eaten. What is it about piranhas that makes them deadly enough to have inspired several Hollywood flicks?

Piranhas are small fish that live in fresh water. They have really sharp teeth and are found in the rivers of South America. They hunt in schools (a group of fish). Just one school can contain as many as 1000 fish.

Because of their sharp teeth, piranha can dig into and consume huge amounts of meat amidst themselves as a group. While they usually feed on other animals, in case of a shortage, a piranha can even feed on their own species to survive.

FAST FACT . . .
Turtles, crocodiles, and dolphins love to feed on piranhas.

FAST FACT . . .
Piranha found in the Venezuela River of South America are referred to as Cribes by the local people.

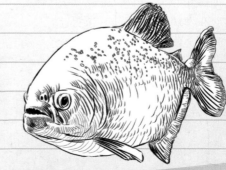

83. MADAGASCAR

Madagascar is teeming with animal species that are not found anywhere else in the world. Amongst them are the world's biggest and smallest chameleons—Parson and Brookesia.

Madagascar broke away from the African subcontinent 165 million years ago, which is probably why the species that survived here haven't been spotted anywhere else in the world. Amongst those species are the largest and the smallest chameleons.

The smallest chameleon is called the Brookesia chameleon. It is hardly 1.18 inches long and is found amidst leaf litter in the rainforest, and also in the dry deciduous forests.

The largest chameleon is the Parson's chameleon, which is 2.28 feet long. It is found along forest streams and in mid- and low-altitude rainforests.

FAST FACT . . .
There are more than 6,000 different types of plants in Madagascar.

FAST FACT . . .
Madagascar also has around 70 species of lemurs.

84. THE ANGLER FISH

The Angler fish isn't very pleasant-looking. But even while it's not the prettiest, its mechanism of trapping its prey is quite amusing. Care to find out what it is?

The angler fish is usually dark gray to dark brown in color, and is most often found in tropical environments. That's the only mundane thing about this fish. What's interesting is how this fish chooses to catch its prey. The angler fish uses a rather sophisticated tool to catch its unsuspecting prey. A fishing rod! At the end of its fishing rod, which dangles right in front of its big and ugly mouth, is a light. A kind of a bulb, which helps Mr Angler attract its prey. When the prey gets attracted to

FAST FACT . . .

The mouths of angler fishes are crescent shaped and are filled with sharp, translucent teeth.

the light, it swims towards it and comes really close. The Angler fish then pounces on it and gobbles it up.

This fish has more than 200 types and some of them are found at the bottom of the sea. A species of angler fish is also found in the Mariana Trench. These carnivorous fish are about 8 inches to 3 feet in length and they weigh around 110 lbs.

FAST FACT . . .

In the deep sea, it's only the female angler fish that has the role of fishing. The males just tag along with the females.

85. GIANT LEATHERBACK TURTLES

The giant leatherback turtles are the largest turtles on Earth. They have been around since the time of the dinosaurs, and have survived this long! But these turtles, who have made it through the last 100 million years, might not survive the next 20.

The leatherback turtles are carnivorous turtles with an average life span of around 45 years. They can grow up to 7 feet, and can weigh as much as 2,000 lbs. They thrive in the waters of Atlantic and Antarctic Oceans and are considered to be the largest turtles on Earth. But while these turtles have faced the near-fatal meteor attack that wiped out the dinosaurs, it seems like they won't be able to face the challenges posed by the modern era. The population of the leatherback turtle is dwindling now. The primary reason for this is the pollution in the ocean.

FAST FACT . . .

Due to the conditions leading towards the decline of the turtle, only one in a thousand leatherback hatchlings survive.

Apart from that, fishing nets that are meant to catch tons and tons of fish can also pose as a death trap for this turtle. There's also severe climate change, which isn't suiting the turtle well.

FAST FACT . . .
The leatherback turtle has been named as California's official marine reptile.

FAST FACT . . .
Leatherback turtles have the longest migration route—about 3700 miles.

Due to all these conditions, scientists believe that without intervention, the leatherback turtle might go extinct in the next 20 years or so.

86. THE KING OF THE JUNGLE

The King of the Jungle is soon turning into the King of Extinction! The population of lions has reduced from 450,000 to 20,000 in the last 50 years. This majestic animal will disappear from the surface of the Earth in the next couple of decades or so if the trend continues.

FAST FACT . . .
Trading lion bones has become a lucrative business in South Africa.

Today, the population of lions stands at barely 20,000.
The main reason for this decline is urbanization, which is causing the lion's natural habitat to get depleted.
Lions are hunted for their skin, and other body parts, which can be sold for large amounts of money.
Several governments are aware of the problem and are trying to put a stop to this by making the hunting of lions a punishable offence. The boundaries of national reserves have also been fenced to prevent poachers from hunting down this wild beast.

FAST FACT . . .
The American lion, the Bali lion, the Cape lion, and the Caspian lion are some of the kinds of lions that have already gone extinct.

87. BULL FROGS

It surely looks like the bullfrogs of Amazon love their home, but while these croaking creatures have a gala time reproducing and increasing their population, they pose a big question about the balance in the ecosystem of the Amazon.

Frogs are creatures that need a moist habitat, and are usually found on the edges of ponds. This is because frogs breathe from their skin, and for this process to take place smoothly, they need to keep their skin moist.

Strangely, the case of the Amazon frogs is a little different. The bullfrogs, first of all, do not belong here. They were imported to the country to satiate people's appetite for frogs' legs, and some farmers introduced the bullfrog into the Amazonian forests.

After settling in their new homes, the bullfrogs realized that they need not hang out exclusively around water. They realized that they could venture a little further and settle down under trees, branches, or big leaves. This is easy in the Amazon because the climate in these forests is really humid, which means that regardless of where the frog is, it remains moist.

Because these frogs aren't staying close to their natural habitat, they easily escape their natural predators, like crocodiles, which means that there is no natural check on their population growth. In fact, the ecosystem has become unbalanced because the population of bullfrogs is overtaking the population of the native frogs of Amazon.

88. PLANKTONS

These are plants that float along with the ocean currents, and the name plankton is derived from the Greek word "planktos," which means "drifter" or "wanderer." Even though not much credit is given to these plants, life on Earth wouldn't exist without them.

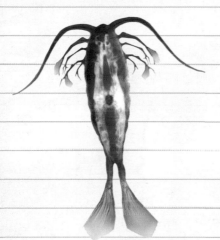

percent of the Earth's surface is covered by oceans. Planktons are present in most parts of these oceans. Several studies have revealed that 50 percent of the oxygen that we breathe has been contributed to the atmosphere by the planktons. Zooplanktons are organisms that feed on planktons. These, in turn, fall prey to other animals and fish in the sea. As you can see, planktons play a very

There are many kinds of planktons that float in water bodies, mainly in oceans. They are diatoms, dinoflagellates, cyanobacteria, green algae, and coccolithophores. Around 70

FAST FACT . . .

Phytoplanktons are planktons that produce oxygen by the process of photosynthesis.

important role in the food chain of the oceans. In fact, it is the plankton that forms the base of food chains in the oceans.

FAST FACT . . .

Due to the oil spills and other pollutants that enter the sea or ocean, plankton blooms are formed. These blooms can sometime turn toxic and destroy ecosystems in the sea.

89. JELLYFISH

Almost everyone would like to turn back time and spend their entire life playing tag. This fantasy of ours is actually a reality for the *Turritopsis nutricula* jellyfish.

The jellyfish becomes free-floating very late in its life. Its life cycle begins when the sperm from the male jelly fish fertilizes the female egg and forms a larva, which floats out and attaches itself to a sturdy surface. It then becomes a stationary polyp, which, over a period of time, grows and becomes a colony of polyps connected by tubes. After a long time, this colony of polyps detaches itself from the sturdy surface and becomes a free-floating jellyfish.

If the jellyfish is very hungry, and hasn't eaten in a long time, it can actually transform back into the single polyp! The aging process thus starts all over again. That's how this particular species of jellyfish could go on living forever. But it doesn't usually happen that way; it usually dies due to an illness, or gets eaten up by some predator first.

FAST FACT . . .

A group of jellyfish is called a bloom or a smack, and they contain about 100,000 jellyfish.

FAST FACT . . .

The sting of the jellyfish nematocytes works even after the jellyfish is dead.

90. THE GOLDEN WATTLE

This large, fluffy, yellow-flowered plant is commonly known as Australia's floral emblem. It's scientific name is *Acacia pycnantha* and it usually blooms in the spring. What makes it so special? Let's find out.

While all these qualities make it a perfectly pleasant plant, what about it qualifies it to become the national floral emblem of Australia? Ask any Australian and you'll get your answer in a jiffy—it symbolizes the two colors present in the Australian flag: green and gold. Now that the Golden Wattle has found its honorary place, it pops up at

FAST FACT . . .
On days of national mourning, Australians wear a sprig of the Golden Wattle.

many social dos and events of national concerns, like awards and ceremonies, and even on the national stamp!

AMAZON RAINFORESTS

HAILSTORMS

GREAT PACIFIC GARBAGE PATCH

ENDANGERED

RECYCLING

PITCHER PLANT

DEAD ZONES

EARTH DAY

GLOBAL WARMING

SATELLITE

RECYCLING

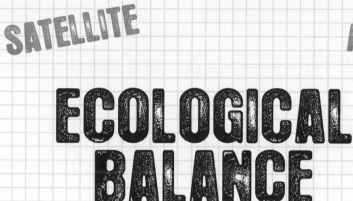

ECOLOGICAL
BALANCE

OZONE LAYER

BEES

APRIL 22

EXTINCTION

91. AMAZON RAINFOREST

Green plants and trees are responsible for the oxygen present on the Earth, and so, areas which have a dense tree cover play a very important role in maintaining the oxygen balance in the world.

Amazonia or the Amazon Rainforest is sprawled over 2,722,000 square miles in the northeastern part of the South American continent. Because Amazonia provides about 20 percent of the oxygen in the world, it's known as the "lungs of our planet."

According to scientists, the Amazon forest comprises of more than half of the species of wildlife in the world. It has 500 kinds of mammals, 175 types of lizards, more than 300 species of reptiles, and about one-third kinds of the birds found all over the world.

The Amazonia that covers more than half of Brazil experiences 9 feet of rain every year and most of the water from rainfall gets used by the thick foliage found in this area.

FAST FACT . . .

The temperature of Amazonia is warm and humid. During summers the average temperature is approximately 79° F.

92. HAILSTORMS

Hailstorms don't pose as great a danger as an earthquake or floods, but the year 2004 revealed that hailstorms can kill, really. So here's an introduction to yet another natural disaster that can take lives.

Hail is formed in the same way as raindrops or snowflakes are formed. Sometimes, the moisture in the clouds solidifies to such a great extent due to the temperature that it doesn't quite melt before pelting down. That's how hail is formed. In 2004, a team of researchers came across a "Skeleton Lake" in India which they found remains of people who had died in 850 A.D. Further research revealed that around 200 people got killed during a hailstorm in 850 A.D.

FAST FACT . . .
An average hailstone has a diameter of 0.19–5.9 inches.

FAST FACT . . .
Hailstones are made in the Cumulonimbus cloud, which is also known as the "thundercloud."

93. THE EARTH DAY

On April 22, you begin to see banners announcing Earth Day and a huge list of things that you can do to make this Earth a better place to live in. We're sure you've noticed. How did this whole fuss around Earth Day begin?

The first Earth Day was celebrated on April 22, 1970, in America. It was Wisconsin Senator Gaylord Nelson who we have to thank for beginning this tradition. It all began in 1872 when J Sterling Morton, a Nebraska pioneer, planted about a million trees—at least that's how the legend goes—on Arbor Day on April 10. After Morton passed away, Arbor Day got shifted to his birthday on April 22. In 1970, Nelson decided to rename this day as Earth Day after he saw the damage caused by humans to nature. What instigated this was the massive oil spill in Santa Barbara, California, that he witnessed in 1969.

On the first Earth Day in 1970, 20 million Americans paraded through streets, parks,

FAST FACT . . .
Earth Day enthusiast, Proctor & Gamble advocates the use of cold water in washing machines which reduces the CO_2 emission.

auditoriums, and theaters to spread awareness about the damage caused by power plants, raw sewage, toxic dumps, pesticides, etc.

On the occasion of Earth Day, people are encouraged to use recycled products, plant trees, reduce pollution, switch off their televisions, and live as close to nature as they can.

FAST FACT . . .
Costa Rica is the happiest country in the world while USA ranks 105th.

94. THE OZONE LAYER

There is a very thin layer of ozone high up in the atmosphere that protects us from the harmful ultraviolet (UV) rays. This layer is present in the stratosphere. Recently, scientists have discovered holes in this ozone layer.

The ozone layer is present at a height of about 10–30 miles from the Earth's surface in the Stratosphere. The ozone layer is essential for human beings because it protects us from harmful UV rays that can cause skin cancer. The ozone layer deflects such rays and sends them back into space.

But for a few years now, scientists have been observing huge holes in the ozone layers. These holes are found above the Arctic and the Antarctic regions. Also, in certain places the ozone layer has thickened. This thickening leads to smog formation, which has been observed in many cities.

When the increased concentration of ozone sneaks into the lower levels of the atmosphere—such as the Troposphere—it reacts with the smoke, dust, and other pollutants, causing smog. It is a phytochemical reaction. Smog can cause respiratory troubles like asthma and bronchitis, and reduce the body's resistance to cold and other lung infections. The imbalance in the ozone layer is due to the increased use of Chloroflurocarbons (CFCs) which is used in refrigerators and fire extinguishers, amongst others modern inventions.

FAST FACT . . .

Ozone is made up of three oxygen atoms (O_3) and is a highly reactive gas.

Oxygen O_2

Ozone O_3

95. PACIFIC GARBAGE

We empty all our waste into the ocean. And yes, all the countries do it. Have you ever thought about where the garbage from the entire world goes? Of course it doesn't evaporate! The waste goes and lodges itself in the Great Pacific Garbage Patch.

This Great Pacific Garbage Patch is situated in the North Pacific Sub Tropical Gyre.

It is not one big patch, but is divided into two parts—the Western and the Eastern Garbage Patch. The Eastern Patch, which floats between Hawaii and California, is said to be larger than Texas City. Imagine — that's the amount of garbage that goes into our oceans. In terms of life in such Garbage Patches, the only form of life is plankton. The spiraling currents of the North Pacific Subtropical

Gyre suck in the garbage from all over. The increasing volume of this Garbage Patch is posing a threat to marine lives.

FAST FACT . . .
The debris in the Great Pacific Garbage Patch has increased over 100 times in the past 40 years.

96. ENDANGERED BEES

The population of bees all over the world is in a decline. While this doesn't sound very alarming, scientists believe that it is an issue to worry about. Some have even said that if bees were to go extinct, humans will disappear from the Earth four years later. But where are the bees going?

On close observation, scientists have found out that the population of bees is decreasing by nearly 80 percent in USA, and by around 25 percent in Germany. While the cause of this is not confirmed yet, some believe that a particular chemical in the pesticides that are being used is to be blamed. The interesting thing is that the chemical is not directly killing the bees. Instead, it's causing the bees to become disoriented and lose their way. When a bee

is not able to come back to its hive, it eventually dies. This is a cause for concern because bees are responsible for the pollination of flowers, and in their absence, there will be no more plants!

FAST FACT . . .
Honeybees know how to calculate angles.

97. THE PITCHER PLANT

Whenever we hear about a carnivorous plant, such as the pitcher plant, we assume that it gobbles up any unsuspecting insect that manages to come near it. But it seems like the diving ant and the pitcher plant seem to have struck a good deal. The pitcher plant, for some reason, refuses to eat this ant.

Such peculiarity has been noticed at the Island of Borneo, situated in the north of Java. In this area, you find colonies where the diving ant and the pitcher plant exist together. On closer inspection, scientists observed that the diving ant was so comfortable with the pitcher plant that it calmly entered it and ate the remains of the half-digested insects in the plant, without any objection from the plant itself!

Experiments were then conducted to solve this mystery and it was found that when the diving ant excretes or dies, it provides the pitcher plant with much-needed nitrogen.

98. SATELLITES

You may have heard about a Hubble telescope that keeps an eye on the Earth from outer space. In a few years' time, we will have a similar satellite that will keep a check on the ecological changes taking place on Earth. Maybe that will make it easier for us to keep a track of our progress.

In recent years, many environmentalists and scientists have been worried about the ecological changes that have been taking place on Earth. From the disappearance of bees to global warming, everything seems to be heading in a downward direction.

FAST FACT . . .
The cost of this NEON project is approximately 300 million US dollars.

To make matters worse, no one has a clear answer about what can be done to stop it. That's why scientists are in the process of developing a device similar to the Hubble telescope that will keep a check on the ecological changes. The project is under way at the National Ecological Network Observatory. If all goes well, it should be ready by 2016!

99. THE GLACIER PARK

Yes, there is such a park, and it is located in Montana, USA. The most disappointing fact is that the number of glaciers in this national park has been reduced from 150 to only about 27.

The Glacier National Park was established on May 11, 1910, in Montana. Apart from the glaciers, this 1800 square miles' stretch of national park contains around 762 lakes and many waterfalls.

While this national park is known for its glaciers, their numbers are dwindling. This is because of global warming and pollution. The glaciers have been slowly but steadily melting.

100. RECYCLING

Switzerland recycles 167 tons of paper per 1,000 people. That's the highest number in the whole world. In the wake of global warming, a lot is being said about saving trees and using recycled paper. Apart from saving trees, recycled paper serves many other purposes too. A peek into its positive effects will make you vouch for it.

In an era where cities are growing rapidly, the amount of deforestation each year is dismal. Moreover, many trees are also sacrificed for the want of paper. Environmentalists from all over the world are requesting people to use recycled paper as that will save trees. Apart from just trees, recycled paper saves a whole load of other things too! Here's a tiny list. One ton of recycled paper can save:

17 trees, 380 gallons of oil, 7,000 gallons of water, 4,000 kilowatts of energy, 3.3 cubic yards of landfill space, and also reduce the greenhouse gas emission by one metric ton of carbon equivalent. Recycled paper should be the new superhero!

101. DEAD ZONES

A dead zone is one that has very low levels of oxygen in its atmosphere. Due to this, living organisms find it hard to survive in such areas. Oceanographers have observed that instances of such zones have been increasing since the 1970s.

A dead zone is basically "hypoxic." This means that the oxygen levels over such zones are very low. Studies reveal that use of plastic, pesticides, and other pollutants that are choking the environment are the cause of this.

When pesticides get washed away into water bodies, they cause phytoplankton to bloom. These blooms are toxic. On consuming such toxic planktons, the zooplanktons die. Phytoplanktons and zooplanktons are responsible for providing the oxygen underwater. Once they die, the oxygen levels dip, and the dissolved oxygen gets used up. One such zone has been found along the Gulf Coasts of North America.

INDEX